The Inside Story

Also by Neil McKenty:

Mitch Hepburn

In the Stillness Dancing: The Journey of John Main

The Inside Story

Journey of a former Jesuit priest and
talk show host towards self-discovery

Neil McKenty

Shoreline

THE INSIDE STORY
Journey of a former Jesuit priest and talk show host towards
self-discovery

Copyright: Neil McKenty, 1997
Cover: Gottschalk + Ash International
Printed in Canada by Imprimerie d'édition Marquis ltée
Published by Shoreline, 23 rue Ste-Anne, Ste-Anne-de-Bellevue,
      Quebec H9X 1L1, phone/fax: 514-457-5733
Dépôt légal: Bibliothèque nationale du Québec &
      The National Library of Canada

Cataloguing in Publication Data

McKenty, Neil, 1924-
      The inside story: journey of a former Jesuit priest and talk show
host towards self-discovery

ISBN 1-896754-01-5

      1. Broadcasters--Québec (Province)--Biography. 2. Depression,
Mental. 3. McKenty, Neil, 1924-   4. Substance abuse. 5. Jesuits--
Canada. I. Title.

BX4668.3.M34A3 1997   791.45'6'092   C96-900038-6

For Catharine

AUTHOR'S NOTE

Why, a friend asked me, are you writing this book? Why describe a journey about toxic religion, sex and celibacy, drinking and depression? Because, I answered simply, the journey led me to a measure of self-discovery and because I believe others will relate to my feelings along the way and perhaps be helped on their own journey towards wholeness. For reasons of privacy I have changed a few names. Many have helped me on this journey but I will only mention here my wife, Catharine, to whom this memoir is dedicated and without whose love and support I should not have survived.

Neil McKenty

We shall not cease from exploration
And the end of all our exploring
Will be to arrive where we started
And know the place for the first time.

T.S. Eliot, *Little Gidding*

CONTENTS

Prelude   13

1. Drinking and Damnation   15

2. Writing and Resentment   29

3. Death and the Jesuits   37

4. Whips and Chains   45

5. The Third Degree   59

6. Cruelty and Paranoia   67

7. Failure and Success   73

8. Priesthood and Sex   79

9. Suicide and Asylum   89

10. Wealthy Widows and Speakers' Corner   97

11. Books and Booze   105

12. Special Olympics and Special Wedding   115

13. Broadcasting and Benedictines   121

14. Clinical Depression   137

15. Spiritual Awakening   145

PRELUDE

Exactly a week before Good Friday in March 1994, a day soft and sunny, Catharine and I left Montreal and drove up the Laurentian Autoroute to the old monastery beside Rivière du Diable in Parc Mont Tremblant. We put on our cross-country skis in the parking lot and set off. I remember feeling almost exhilarated as we skied along through the pine trees, the wind in our face, the branches tracing tapestries on the snow which glittered in the sunshine.

Then Saturday morning I plunged again into a bottomless shaft of gloom and dread. I had never before felt so helpless and hopeless, so sunk in a curious state of perturbed paralysis. From my couch, I told Catharine I felt terrible, but she lived with her own dread and knew there was nothing she could do about mine. She had an appointment at Unitas, the meditation centre on Mount Royal above Pine Avenue, but was afraid to leave the house. However, in a way she could neither justify nor understand, she felt compelled to go. She locked the door behind her. I was alone.

I wanted to sink more deeply into the shaft of darkness and oblivion that would give me relief from this pain, this cancer of the soul. I wanted to sink into the soft nothingness of death. Suddenly, a flash like heat lightning lit up the oppressive gloom in my head. Momentarily I glimpsed the flames of hell and damnation flickering the way the Catholic Church had painted them to me as a little boy. I could feel the forbidden sex of my Jesuit years and taste the warming gurgle of alcohol melting the ice in my soul. Then the moment of clarity vanished. The clouds rolled in and the tapes in my head, the suicide tapes, began playing again.

I had long since given up the idea of a gun or death by drowning. The tape now playing was about a plunge onto the tracks of the Montreal métro. I knew this would be messy for me and for those who survived me, especially Catharine. But I was no longer thinking of others. My inner being was like an inkwell overflowing with black thoughts of nothing but myself.

I pushed off the blanket and got up from the couch, my body leaden. I watched my movements as though I was a spectator in a dark cinema. Slowly and laboriously, I found a pencil and a piece of paper and wrote a suicide note: "Dearest Catharine, I think you will be better off without me. Love, Neil." Then I folded the paper, my own obituary notice, and placed it carefully on the floor just inside the front door.

1

DRINKING AND DAMNATION

Hastings, where Stafford and I grew up in the Depression years, is a village on the Trent River in southern Ontario. In the 1930s, it was a village of nearly a thousand people, twenty miles from Peterborough, which was famous for its lift locks and Quaker Oats "shot from guns." Whenever our parents took us to Peterborough for an outing, Stafford and I always peered down the Otonabee River towards the Quaker Oats factory and listened for the guns. As for Hastings, it had three claims to fame: the Breithaupt Company where the men tanned leather; the many tourists who came from the United States and Toronto to camp and catch fish, especially pickerel; and the sports teams - hockey, baseball and lacrosse.

Hastings' Main Street ran partly along the Trent River and contained what one would expect in most Ontario villages then - two restaurants, a hotel, two drugstores, a variety shop, a Royal Bank branch, the untidy office of *The Hastings Star*, Pettigrew's barber shop which occasionally displayed the sign "Back in 5 minutes," a smoky pool hall where we played eight ball (and if we were caught, there was hell to pay), a gas station and garage, a realty office run by the village reeve, a bakery with sweets and dead flies in the window, Tim Coughlan's hand-operated telephone exchange (where the operators, all girls, plugged in their calls, then yacked to the boys who were always hanging around), and two hardware stores.

My father, Arthur Joseph (always Arthur to my mother, Art to most of his customers and A.J. to many of his friends), owned one of the hardware stores, by far the best-stocked and the most profitable. It was situated on a corner of the main intersection in town, and was across from the Royal Hotel - which was more popular for its beverage room than for its food. My father was a big man, just under six feet, with an imposing almost military presence, perhaps from having served overseas in the First World War. He had a booming voice and a loud laugh and smoked cigars. Successful as a hardware merchant during the Depression and as a tinsmith, which was his trade, he was well respected in the community. He was active in Hastings' separate school board, the Roman Catholic church of which he was a devout communicant, and the baseball team, which he helped financially. Some would call my father hail-fellow-well-met, others a diamond in the rough. Whatever the precise words, my father filled a large space. You knew he was there.

My mother, Irene, short, slightly plump, with a warm and welcoming smile, filled her own space in her own way. Born on a farm near Norwood in April 1889, she was a daughter of William Shea and Bridget McCarthy. Tranquil, gentle and friendly, she had become a school teacher during the First World War. People liked her and she made them feel at home. She had an enjoyment of simple delights. Wearing a floppy white summer hat and a white dress spangled with bright flowers, she would serve tea on our spacious verandah to friends and relatives, including her favourite cousin, Mona Shoobert, from Toronto. Like my father, she had a deep faith in God and was active in the church, especially in the Catholic Women's League, where she had been parish president. Someone once described Irene as a classy lady. She was - with her faith, loving devotion to her family, generosity to her friends, and love of her home.

Our home was one of the largest and most attractive in Hastings, a three-storey Victorian house, painted robin's-egg blue with white gingerbread trim, set in a large green lawn. On hot summer nights, my parents often slept on the roomy second-storey screened porch overlooking the street. Our back yard, studded with berry bushes, was so spacious that we turned it into a sports field. Our friends Tim Coughlan, Phil MacDonald and other neighborhood kids played on a baseball diamond, a scaled-down rugby field, an ice hockey rink which my father built, and even a boxing ring which we used until my grandfather Shea, who lived with us then, said was too dangerous and we reluctantly had to dismantle it.

My mother's taste, bright but delicate, made our house colourful and comfortable. She was proud of its classical architecture and its quality workmanship, especially evident in the trim cabinets and oak floors. My father took a special interest in the hardwood floors in the dining room and the parlour (which held Mother's piano), sanding, varnishing and polishing them until they shone like glass.

On Sunday afternoons my father cooked the meat, especially succulent when it was a roast of venison on a bracing fall day. Venison was often given to him by his former hunting buddies. We usually celebrated birthdays with our friends the Coughlan and MacDonald kids, who helped us blow out the candles on the rich, dark chocolate birthday cake. Mother was an excellent cook. Halloween was a night of more candies and candles (except for the night when three of us teenagers knocked over an outhouse down by the river, unfortunately with a Toronto tourist inside).

Most of our neighbours and friends, I am sure, perceived our home as a warm and happy place. And it would have been except for one drawback - my father's drinking. His drinking, habitual and heavy, changed him from a congenial husband and dad into a morose, sometimes frightening bully. Alcohol would alter our lovely Victorian residence on Bridge Street from a home where there was happiness and love into a house where too often there was tension and anxiety, the kind of anxiety that early on seeped into my bones and lodged like a jagged stone in the pit of my stomach.

My father was born in Madoc, a village northeast of Peterborough, on November 20, 1882. Both his parents died, of diphtheria I believe, before he was nine years old. He was brought up by my mother's parents, William and Bridget Shea. My grandfather Shea had been a successful farmer, then a popular streetcar conductor in Peterborough until he retired. Every day after school my father learned the tinsmithing trade, and worked for a hardware man and tinsmith named Rorke in Norwood. The only time I ever heard my father cry, many years later, was the night he heard that his old boss, whom he always called Mr. Rorke, had died. Shortly after the First World War began, my father left Rorke's Hardware to enlist in an infantry battalion. He was thirty-one years old.

During the months he was overseas fighting in the trenches of France, my father kept up a steady correspondence, one or two letters weekly, with his future wife. Irene, then twenty-five, was teaching elementary school at Gravenhurst in the Muskokas. Dad was grateful for all the packages Irene and her family were sending him, especially the supply of chewing tobacco, but he thought she was overly concerned about his safety.

"I wish," he wrote Irene's mother at the end of 1916, "she would not worry so much about me." And to his future bride directly:

"Because I do not write long letters, do not cut yours off short or if you run a week without one don't be uneasy because if anything happens to me your father will get a cable-gram at once."

In several of these wartime letters written at the beginning of 1917, my father speaks of going to mass and how much solace that gave him. "The church is beautiful but old Fritz punched a few holes in the roof.... Our priests - and we have two - are just fine men.... And believe me it is a great comfort to be able to go to mass." Later he alludes to a drinking spree when he was on leave in Southampton. "No, I did not go to see *Birth of a Nation* in Southampton. I forget now what we did but I think we had a good time. Rather a vague excuse, isn't it? Well, I remember once you said a fellow had a White Horse so I think we were trying to drink him up."

My father's greatest frustration was that Irene could read more in the newspapers about the war than he was permitted to tell her, and even then only in vague terms. "When the trenches are very wet we are given big rubber boots right up to the hips. But I would hate to do a two-hundred yard dash in them ... Christmas night [1916] I want to forget forever." But he promised Irene he would make up for his lack of news. "You see if I could tell you events from one day to the other I could write a dozen pages. But I will tell you all some day."

Arthur returned from the war, and he and Irene were married in Peterborough in October 1922. I was born in 1924. We moved to Hastings in 1925 when my father bought the hardware store. Whatever he told Irene after he returned from the war, he never told me anything except that war was hell and to stay out of it. However, I gleaned this much from my mother over the years: he had fought in the mud in the trenches at Passchendaele and Vimy Ridge (his battalion had been inspected by King George V on horseback), he was wounded while carrying an injured comrade to safety, was decorated for bravery (my mother kept the medal) and was invalided home in late 1917. I also understood that my father's battalion had been caught in a surprise German gas attack. Whether the gas affected him in any permanent way I do not know.

What I do know is that my father's heavy drinking after the war and after we moved to Hastings affected me seriously. He never drank at home, nor did anyone else except for Grandpa Shea who took an occasional snifter of brandy for medicinal reasons. Dad never drank on Sunday, never drank socially and never, so far as I was aware, became drunk in the sense he could not function. But his drinking was a central pattern in his life and it left scars on my own.

Dad drank beer. He drank almost daily in the dark and dingy beverage room of the Royal Hotel, reeking with the acrid smell of smoke and stale urine, its small tables pock-marked with cigarette burns. It was directly across Main Street from the corner store with the big sign, "A.J. McKenty & Sons Hardware." I always knew when my dad was over at the hotel drinking - the store would be closed or he would have asked a customer friend to look after it while he ran across to the hotel "to fix a leaky faucet." And sometimes he went up the River Road to Al Scriver's, the town's bootlegger and poet. I could always tell when he was drinking at Al Scriver's because his old Dodge touring car, the roof sometimes piled high with tools and eaves troughing, would be parked outside for everyone to see. I would always feel a shiver of shame and apprehension.

My dad's habitual drinking did something to him and it did something to me. The alcohol made him moody, irritable and somehow menacing. Never once did he do anything physical to any of us (except with the strap). Once, when he *wasn't* drinking, he bounded out of Walter Hubbell's barber chair, all lathered up, ready to throttle a stringer for *The Toronto Star* who had written that Dad thought most Toronto tourists were cheapskates - which in fact he did. His drinking frightened me, angered me and depressed me; resentment of his drinking ran through my system like a low-grade fever.

I still remember walking down from the two-room red brick Catholic grade school, Our Lady of Mount Carmel, at the top of the hill across from the town hall and the white cenotaph, and into my dad's store at the end of the school day. As soon as I walked past the fishing tackle and the binder twine and the nail kegs, I would look for Dad behind the counter near the cash register. If he had been drinking, it would be immediately obvious from the expression on his face and by the bitter smell of beer. If he had not, my anxiety would melt like an ice cube in the sun. If, more likely, he had, my heart would sink. Through those early school years I lived on an emotional roller coaster and there was no way I knew to get off.

It is difficult to measure the effect of my father's drinking on my own personality then and on my own battle with alcohol later on. However, the result was confusion. On the one hand, I felt ashamed and embarrassed. Sometimes I suspected even our closest friends and relatives looked down on Dad, and on all of us, because he drank too much or was, as I am now convinced, an alcoholic. On the other hand, I resented these hostile judgments by others and felt an obligation to defend him in public. Gradually the tension inherent in this split became more acute.

There was another problem. I couldn't reconcile my father's drinking with the strict code of behaviour he preached and indeed frequently practiced. He was a rigid disciplinarian ("Eat your Brussels sprouts and/or string beans or sit at the table [sometimes for two hours] until you do.") A family friend once said Dad did not know how to relate to children. Was this because he had his own so late? He was forty-two and my mother thirty-five when I was born. He was forty-four when my brother, Stafford, came along. In addition to his disciplinarian bent, my father was a strict Roman Catholic from a rigid Irish background, as was my mother. Religion played a central role in our home and our school and it permeated our lives. Our religion in those years, as I think about it now, was as pervasive in our lives as alcohol was and about as depressing. In those early years of the 1930s, my experience of Roman Catholicism, soured by Irish scrupulosity, was not a positive one. It was, if anything, destructive.

I can't think of a more vivid example of this than preparing for our first confession in the junior room of the Catholic school with its black box stove blazing. I suspect the year was 1932, the year the Lindbergh baby was kidnapped and murdered - the first news story I remember. My first grade teacher was stout red-haired Miss McMahon, a devoted and conscientious teacher, and I was seven years old. I also remember the first day of school when Mother walked me in my short pants to the door to find that all my classmates were wearing long pants, an occurrence I found embarrassing and deeply resented.

Day after day, Miss McMahon drummed into us the seriousness of confession. What I still remember is that she emphasized the stern justice of God and the eternity of hell. We didn't spend much time on venial sin, a fuzzy concept like pinching your brother's teddy bear. But mortal sin, that was a different kettle of fish altogether. Committing a mortal sin without forgiveness in the confessional could catapult you into hell forever.

Hell was described in horrendous terms by the Redemptorist missionaries who came once a year to give a week's mission in the parish. These Redemptorists were specialists in religious terrorism. First, they would describe hell as an enormous oven raging with flames from which there was no escape, ever. I got the message, but in case I didn't, the Redemptorist missionary spelled it out. If I committed a mortal sin and didn't get to confession before I was killed by a truck, God would, that very instant, consign me to hell. "Now imagine," thundered the Redemptorist in a booming voice (all missionaries who came to our parish had booming voices), "a bird flying over a sand beach a thousand miles long, a hundred miles wide and fifty feet deep. This bird flies over the beach just once a year. And each year the bird picks up just one grain of sand. By the time," roared the Redemptorist, "the sand will be all gone, eternity in the ovens of hell will be just beginning."

This description of a fiery and everlasting inferno may seem ridiculous now but it wasn't ridiculous to me, seven years old, in 1932. It was God's own truth backed by the power and panoply of the Catholic Church as symbolized in my little world by my parents, my teachers, the parish priest, the Redemptorist missionary and any other priest I might meet - some of whom had a more gentle and loving message. There were lists of mortal sins, most of them sexual. Masturbation, usually described as "touching yourself," was at the top of the list. It was at a softball game that I first heard about masturbation and how it worked - this from an older boy who many years later committed suicide. I well remember the first and only time my mother caught me masturbating. I had slept in late on a Saturday morning and she walked into my bedroom unexpectedly. She was horrified; I was ashamed. She ordered me out of bed, grabbed the sheets and took them to be washed.

Confessing masturbation was about as pleasant as having a tooth drilled. We went to confession every Saturday afternoon to Hastings' one parish priest. Despite the darkness of the confessional box (like an upended coffin) and the thick wire screen separating us, the priest soon got to know me. If one masturbated regularly (which I did) and if one confessed this mortal sin regularly (which I also did), the priest would threaten to refuse one absolution (which he eventually did). This left me in a dreadful slough of shame and fear. Either I would not go up with my family to receive holy communion at Sunday mass, which was not a viable choice because my parents would want to know why, or I could go to communion without being absolved from my mortal sin of masturbation and, in the process, commit another sin of a still more heinous kind called a sacrilege. This meant that I had somehow

crucified Christ again and was consigned to the regions of the damned -
a terrain I would explore more fully years later in the novels of Graham
Greene.

In those days I was often in this predicament, frozen with fear of
my parents and dread of eternal damnation. There was one way out -
convince a friend to give me a ride to a neighbouring parish so I could
go to confession to a priest who did not know that I was an habitual
masturbator. That way I could avoid the wrath of my parents and the
retribution of God. I still remember the feeling of relief when an
unfamiliar priest released me from the fears of sacrilege and damnation,
and remember walking from the dark confessional out into the
sunshine, as welcome as a warm beach after an icy swim.

But, back to our first confession. For weeks we prepared for it, with
warnings by Miss McMahon, reinforced weekly by more admonitions
from the parish priest, that if in our confession we forgot any mortal
sins like touching ourselves, we risked hellfire. When we were finally
ready at the age of six or seven to make our first confession, I waited
in line in the parish church with my friends, trying to hear what the
others were whispering. In the confessional box, feeling queasy, I
mumbled what I thought were a few sins, received absolution and
stumbled out.

But I still felt tormented. Had I made a good confession? Had I
forgotten something? Did the priest hear me? Did he understand what
I said? Would God forgive me or would I commit a sacrilege? And the
worst was still to come. Walking across the Trent River bridge on the
way home from my first confession in the spring of 1932, I got into an
argument with a boy my own age from the public school. I don't
remember what the argument was about but I remember I said "hell." I
was petrified because I knew that saying "hell" was a sin, perhaps a
mortal sin. And if I didn't confess this new sin, I would commit a
sacrilege on my first holy communion morning.

I was paralyzed with fear and shame. I couldn't not go to first
communion with my class. And I couldn't go with a mortal sin on my
soul. Finally I told my mother. She told my father when he returned
home for supper. He then telephoned the parish priest who agreed that
next morning Dad would take me to church early so that I could go to
confession again. I didn't sleep all night. Next morning the priest met
me in the sacristy and heard my new confession. He was very kind. I
had avoided a sacrilege.

I don't think I ever found confession a very constructive experience and I have long since given it up as a regular practice. But in those early years from age seven on, confession was the equivalent of taking a dose of salts or senna tea, which we had to do every Friday night to "get cleaned out." To the accompanying gastric pains was now added spiritual diarrhea.

If confession with its sulfurous stench of mortal sin and risk of hellfire was the most upsetting of my early religious experiences, there were other positive ones to balance the ledger. The parish priest, Father Paul Costello, who had married my parents in Peterborough, chose me to be an altar boy. This meant learning to serve mass, to speak some Latin, and to assist at weddings and funerals - with a chance of generous tips for the former. Even in a village parish with a hundred families or so, some of the liturgical functions, especially those in Holy Week, were as intricate and precise as a ballet on ice. At Sunday's high mass there was a processional from the sacristy up the main aisle, the priest sprinkling the congregation with holy water, and altar boys swinging the censers with their aromatic fumes. There were bows, genuflections and pirouettes. I was elated to be part of this liturgical drama.

I was even more elated to be appointed head altar boy. This gave my parents a good deal of pride and it gave me a sense of superiority - which was threatened one Sunday night outside the post office. Another altar boy and I got into a fist fight about which of us should be master of ceremonies at the next high mass. It was during these years, the late 1930s, when I was in my mid-teens, that I heard the first intimations that I might have a vocation to the priesthood. This affected me in two ways: it made me feel special and important and it also made me feel uncomfortable. How could I appear so religious to others and at the same time feel so uneasy and anxious deep down inside myself? This split became more uncomfortable after Father J.J. Garvey was appointed to Our Lady of Mount Carmel parish in Hastings in 1940. Even my mother, a faithful Catholic with a strong and simple faith, had some reservations about Father Garvey.

Father Garvey was one of those pinched Irish Catholic priests who saw himself in the place of Christ and his congregation in the place of sinners needing continuous redemption. He was a hypochondriac who enjoyed indifferent health, and a neurotic who took out his suffering on his parishioners. For the most part, his Sunday sermons were condemnations of too much boozing, too much sexual hanky-panky and complaints about lack of money for the parish - in spite of which he built a new rectory, palatial by Hastings' standards. One time Father Garvey had the church doors locked just before Sunday mass began because he said that too many parishioners were coming late. When Sunday collections declined, he threatened to read out the names of those who were giving less or nothing at all. And he did.

One hot summer Sunday, a tourist from Toronto, a young banker, left the church after Father Garvey's sermon. I discovered later that Father Garvey's excoriating the abuse of alcohol had made the banker so thirsty he went out to the local bootlegger's for a drink. In catechism classes Father Garvey was a specialist on impure thoughts. If, for example, you thought about touching a girl's breasts and took pleasure in that thought (presumably if your "peter" as we called it then so much as tingled), that was a mortal sin. And if you couldn't get to Father Garvey or some other priest to confess before you were hit by a truck and killed, you would go straight to perdition for all eternity - which we all knew was a hell of a long time because we remembered what the Redemptorist priest had told us about the bird picking up the sand on the beach.

I could usually deal with the tingle of impure thoughts in my next confession. But sometimes, for me, Father Garvey's moral strictures had more public and humiliating consequences. For instance, he forbade going to the movies during Lent. Hastings had neither a movie theatre nor a high school. In 1939 I had begun high school in Campbellford and a school bus would take us the ten miles there and back. Occasionally, if everybody on the bus agreed, the bus driver would stay in Campbellford after school so we could see a film at the local cinema. I remember after the Second World War started, how proud and elated I was to see Jimmy Cagney in *Captains of the Clouds*, a thrilling film about the Royal Canadian Air Force. But then Lent arrived, and our group wanted to stay for a film. My father, obeying the Church and Father Garvey, ordered me to vote against staying to see the film. I was both angry and frightened but I obeyed him and the bus didn't stay and nobody saw the film. Several of my fellow students berated both me and my father. But I felt I had to defend him in public and I did. Still, I resented him and felt alienated from my fellow students on the bus.

Like the anxiety at the pit of my stomach, this alienation, feeling different from others, had been there from the beginning - never more

24

so than one hot August day when I was seven or eight sitting on the steps of the hardware store. Across the corner in front of the red brick Royal Bank building, a group of farmers were smoking their pipes, perhaps discussing the case of the Lindbergh baby. Along the main street a group of kids, including my brother Stafford, were on their way to a swim at Hank Scriver's boathouse - where Hank made some of the best birch bark canoes in all of Ontario. Some tanned tourists in their shorts passed in front of me on their way to Tim Coughlan's drugstore and the bakery shop. I felt the warmth of the summer sun on my bare arms, but I didn't feel the warmth of the tourists passing by or the kids going swimming. I didn't feel part of them. I felt I was sitting alone inside a bell jar. I couldn't reach out to touch them and they couldn't reach in to touch me. It was a lonely experience, this feeling of being different from others, and it stayed with me, off and on, for most of my life.

Eventually I realized that I must anaesthetize this interior feeling of dis-ease and discomfort, so I decided that since I was different from my peers, I would show them - I would be better than they were. I embarked on a course that led to years of striving and competitiveness, with all the stress and strain those involved.

Being better than others was ineffective as a strategy for success unless it was noticed by others. So I set out to be noticed. Being head altar boy fitted the blueprint. So did coming first in my class which, under pressure from my parents, my priest, my teachers and myself, I managed to do fairly easily during my grade school years. The most visible success of my campaign to be recognized occurred at age nine in the fall of 1934, the fall that Mother drove with Dad and some friends to Campbellford to hear the charismatic Liberal leader, Mitch Hepburn, at a political meeting. That year my teacher, Miss McMahon, chose me to enter the local oratorical contest. This was indeed a feather in my cap. No one in the junior room of the Catholic school had ever been chosen before. The local winner would go to the regional finals and the winners of those to the provincial finals in Toronto.

There was also a religious subtext to this oratorical contest. Hastings was a predominately Protestant village with a strong Orange flavour. On the twelfth of July, leather-lunged Protestant ministers came from as far away as Toronto to flay the Pope, the whore of Babylon, at the local baseball field. After listening to the papists being denounced, we Catholic kids hung around the Orange parade to watch

"King Billy" on his white horse, then ate as much free "orange" ice cream as we could. Dad had taught us to respect all Protestants, as well as the only Jew in the village, a strange man (we thought) with a bushy grey beard and a little black handkerchief on his head. Dad often reminded Stafford and me that many of his customers were Orangemen and if it weren't for them our hardware store would go broke. Every year, as a family, we attended the annual dinners in the Protestant church basements. I have never found the equal of their pies - raspberry, apple and pumpkin, lathered with freshly whipped cream. And on November 11, I would stand rigidly at attention beside my father as the Last Post sounded beside the cenotaph at a mainly Protestant service. This was Dad's only public remembrance of the war. Still and all, we believed that all Protestants would go to hell unless they had the good fortune, maybe on their death bed, to become Catholics.

To some degree, the oratorical contest reflected these religious animosities. The contestants were from the large public Protestant school and the small separate Catholic school. Usually the winner was from the Protestant school. The occasional Catholic victory was attributed to prayers to the Blessed Virgin and was viewed by many as a triumph for the Pope and for Rome. From the outset, Dad was concerned that I not let down our side and make a fool of myself and of him. I had chosen as my topic the life of Sir Wilfred Laurier. Already I was interested in history, especially the career of Franklin Roosevelt. But my teacher and my mother vetoed the choice of Laurier because they thought I didn't know enough about him, a quite reasonable judgement. Instead they wanted me to speak on the topic "When My Grandfather Was A Boy." And that is what I did.

My grandfather, William Shea, my mother's father, was in his eighties then, a spare man over six feet tall with a trim white moustache. He smoked a pipe and occasionally had a spot of brandy with one of his friends. He could be found hour after hour on the bridge over the Trent River or sitting quietly on the dam above the water foaming in the sluiceways, fishing for pickerel, a treat my mother would cook, fresh and tasty, for supper. I liked Grandpa and felt he took pride in my accomplishments. Chuckling as he tamped and smoked his pipe, he would tell us stories about days in a bygone Canada, stories that often made us laugh. But Grandfather Shea had his own ideas about the way we should do things. He would never permit us to call our favourite cousin "Bill" Moore. It had to be "William." And later on when a group of us put up the boxing ring in our back yard, he strode out, cane at the ready, and slashed the ring to pieces, saying he didn't take with boxing for young boys. When Mother and Miss McMahon were helping me put together my speech, I had long talks with Grandpa about his early days on the farm before he became a streetcar conductor in Peterborough.

As the date for the oratorical contest approached, my father became more and more concerned. One day at noon after we had eaten a heavy meal of salt pork, mashed potatoes and rice pudding (we always ate dinner at noon except on Sundays), Dad told me to go into the parlour, where he sat down and asked me to recite my speech for him. I refused. He insisted. I continued to resist until I burst into tears, shaking with fear, anger and resentment. As I recall now, Mother remained in the kitchen. She was not a passive woman but she was a pacifist. She wanted to keep the peace and not rock the boat. Perhaps in some way she was in awe of my father or even afraid of him. (I remember cringing in the back seat of the car when his impatient efforts to teach my mother to drive verged on bullying.) Did I resent Mother's not standing up to Dad when he was badgering me about my speech? I'm not sure. Perhaps she felt getting involved would only make matters worse. In any event, she did not intervene, if indeed she understood what was going on.

At the time, I'm sure I didn't understand what was going on myself. Why wouldn't I recite my speech for my father in the parlour when he asked me to? Was I too embarrassed, too nervous, afraid of forgetting a passage? Was I trying to get back at him on some other issue entirely, such as his drinking? Or was a broader and deeper dynamic at work in this contest of wills? Was I attempting all by myself to stand up to his raw intimidation, to get out, even briefly, from under his oppressive control? And if that was the case, what motivated me, even enveloped in terror, to make such a stand except a dim realization that if I didn't risk it I wouldn't survive? Whatever the dynamic at work, I didn't utter a word of my speech and my father finally gave up.

A short time later I delivered my speech about Grandpa before a town hall packed with supporters from the Catholic and Protestant schools. Competing against eight other candidates, I won first place, thus saving the honour of Rome and pleasing Dad who sweated profusely during the entire evening. This was my first big public triumph, yet despite being victorious, I felt curiously drained and dissatisfied as though my expectations had not been quite met and the good things people were saying about me I did not believe.

2

WRITING AND RESENTMENT

As long as I can remember, I was interested in writing. In 1936, in the senior grade of the separate school, I wrote a long essay on Francisco Franco and the Spanish Civil War. Of course I defended Franco because all the Catholics I knew, including my parents, were praying he would defeat the godless communists. Usually my father took a hard line against communists and that other godless group, the "international bankers," a code name for wealthy Jews who, some believed, controlled the world through the banks. One of those who believed it was the famous radio priest, Father Charles E. Coughlin. In a golden voice as rich and rolling as an organ, Father Coughlin excoriated the international bankers every Sunday afternoon on his radio network originating at the Shrine of the Little Flower in Royal Oak, Michigan. And every Sunday afternoon without fail we had to listen with our father to this spellbinding preacher who fought for the underdog in the middle of the Depression - a stance that appealed to Dad. And we continued to listen every Sunday until Coughlin, a demagogue and a rabid anti-Semite, was removed from the airwaves by his own religious superiors in the spring of 1942.

It was during Father Coughlin's heyday that my interest in radio and writing began to grow. Soon after I began classes at Campbellford High School, my English teacher, Kate Ferris, a tall angular spinster who taught the parsing of sentences as precisely as others might teach figure skating, stopped beside my desk one day and said quietly, "You should work at your writing. You have a flare for it."

I wanted a public forum for my work, because if it wasn't in public it wasn't worth doing; if it wasn't noticed it didn't happen. I was fifteen. The Peterborough Examiner, under editor Robertson Davies, was becoming one of the country's most distinguished newspapers, and I decided I wanted a job. Unfortunately, the fact that I was interested in writing was not enough to convince them to hire me. But help came from an unexpected source. Berk Boyle had written for *The Examiner* and *The Toronto Star* as a sideline when he had lived in Hastings and was working for my dad in the hardware store. When Berk decided to move to Peterborough and go into journalism full time, he asked me if I was interested in a job. I jumped at the chance. *The Examiner* hired me to be a stringer covering the Hastings area.

Being a newspaper stringer in Hastings was like being a minnow in the Trent River. But that wasn't the point. The point was that I was the *only* minnow in the river. I was not only being noticed but was developing some kind of autonomy, breaking out, even fleetingly, from the magnetic field of my father's control. I covered village council meetings, sports events, accidents, fires, runaway horses and Sunday afternoon teas, not to mention lawn bowling tournaments in which both my parents were keen participants. If the reeve of Hastings wanted to see his name in the paper, he called me. If Mrs. Stubbs on the Norwood Road wanted her friends to know she had entertained the Turners from Asphodel, she gave me the information.

I was paid ten cents a columnar inch for hard news (such as a fisherman from Ohio catching a record-breaking muskellunge) or three cents a columnar inch for the personal stuff (Mrs. Stubbs and Mrs. Turner). As soon as I was old enough to drive, I bought an old Dodge touring car for thirty dollars in partnership with my closest friend, Tim Coughlan. The car (whose leaking gas tank we tried to patch with bubble gum) had an enormous windshield. I went to the office of *The Hastings Star* and ordered a large sign. The sign, which I attached to the windshield, read "Press." Everybody in Hastings and its environs knew I was the local reporter for *The Examiner*.

One frigid afternoon in January 1940, Mother met me at our door after the school bus dropped me off. She told me the sad news - the first young man from Hastings had been killed in the war. It was Bud Richardson, serving in the Air Force. He had been a star athlete, especially in the Hastings softball league. His death in action would be a terrible blow to our little town. I grabbed a notebook, put on another sweater against the sub-zero weather and walked the three miles through the snowbanks to the farmstead home of Bud Richardson's parents. I hadn't known Bud Richardson well, but as I walked, I thought of the young athlete we had cheered on the playing field and felt a deep sense of loss. At the farmhouse I talked to Bud's parents about their son and borrowed their only picture of him in uniform. In spite of the circumstances, I enjoyed talking with the Richardsons. I had learned much listening to farm people chewing the fat about politics, prices and crops as we all sat on bails of binder twine around the glowing pot-bellied stove in front of the nail kegs in Dad's hardware store. Bud Richardson's death in action and his picture and story in *The Examiner* brought the war home to Hastings in a personal way. I was there to record it - an experience I will never forget.

Every day before supper I would wait for the bus from Peterborough with its hot-off-the-press copies of *The Examiner*, and would feverishly look through the paper to see if the article I had written had made it into print. Often it had, which would provide a boost to my ego, until Dad would say or do something to sour this elation.

After having finished first in my entrance exams in Hastings, I had started to travel by bus to Campbellford High School in the fall of 1938 when I was thirteen. My dad was uneasy about this change. "I hear," he remarked to others (which was often the way I received information), "that there's humping in the bushes over the lunch hour." I wasn't sure what the words meant but they made me uncomfortable, partly because I thought those to whom my father had made them were laughing at me.

Still, the four years I spent at Campbellford High School from 1938 to 1942 were relatively happy ones as far as school was concerned, despite the movie episode on the bus. I made friends with some of the students, and got on fairly well with most of my teachers, particularly Jean Tubbs who encouraged my interest in history and current events. I was never a natural athlete but did my best in rugby, field events such as high jumping, and hockey - where I played goal because I couldn't skate too well. By putting in long study hours, much of it memorization, I managed to stay in the top half dozen or so students in my class.

At home, however, the tension continued. The main cause was my father's drinking, which kept me in an intermittent state of apprehension and anger. The tension, which affected the whole family, was especially upsetting at the evening meal when Dad, after a day's imbibing, would be unusually truculent and argumentative. Some dinner guests remember him yelling and being extremely disagreeable in the evening. His arguments with my mother's uncle, Dan McCarthy, a pious gentle man, finally drove Uncle Dan from the house. He moved to Peterborough and never returned. Not even the lovely garden Uncle

Dan had created during the years he lived with us could tempt him back.

Increasingly, Dad resented the fact that Mother's father, Grandpa Shea, had been living with us for so many years. I am sure that finances played a part in this resentment as I believe that Grandpa helped to buy our house. Dad tried to get Grandpa to move to the home of his other daughter, Geraldine, in Havelock. I can still see Grandpa, his white hair neatly barbered, staring at his plate, ignoring Dad's barbs while Mother, serving sausages and mashed potatoes, timidly tried to diffuse the tension. After supper my father, morose and still smelling sourly of booze, would go into the living room, stretch out on the couch, and sleep with stentorian snoring for two or three hours until he awoke refreshed and in a much lighter mood, often joking and laughing before going to bed. This scene was played over and over until Grandpa's death in 1939.

In addition to Dad's drinking, my parents' attitude toward discipline sometimes had its own depressing effect. My father told us many times that the Church came first, the school second, my mother third - and a transgression against any one of the three would be doubly punished by him. Kept in a closet was a thick ugly strap of grey mottled leather that resembled the hide of a snake. One late winter afternoon my mother telephoned my father at the store about some disobedience on my part. He came home immediately, told me to roll up my sleeves and strapped me vigorously on both hands. On another occasion Mother sewed up the pockets on my pants so I would keep my hands out of them. Swearing was another taboo. Once Miss McMahon washed my mouth out with soap in front of the class because I allegedly swore at Rosie Crowley during recess. In fact I hadn't.

My emotional confusion was compounded by what appeared to me to be my father's inconsistency, if not hypocrisy. He preached a hard religious line but he drank excessively almost every weekday. He was president of the parish Holy Name Society but sometimes I would walk into the store and hear him cursing and swearing in the back of the tinsmith shop. Once when I was small, Dad took me skating at the open air rink down near the tannery. In the change shack warmed by a roaring fire in the sub-zero weather, he was tying my skates. Suddenly he looked up and gruffly told a group of boys and young men to stop their swearing. There was a sickening silence. I felt like crawling underneath the stove.

My feeling of being different was accentuated when I considered some of the other prominent Catholic families in Hastings, such as the Coughlans and the MacDonalds. Tim Coughlan was our druggist, J.A. MacDonald our doctor, both capable, friendly men with large families. I envied these families because I thought they were freer and happier than we were. When I visited their homes, I experienced a feeling of liberation. I also envied them because I thought they were wealthier than we. For some reason I always feared Dad was going bankrupt. Actually, considering the Depression, he had a good business. One reason for my misapprehension may have been that he had assigned me to take the day's daily deposits to the bank. I would sneak a look at the bank book, where the balance never seemed to increase much, so I concluded we were just staying a step ahead of the bailiff. It was only much later that I discovered the difference between a current account and a savings account. It may also say something about our relationship that I never discussed my concerns with either of my parents.

As I moved through my early teens and high school, I looked out on a world that appeared to me grey and threatening. The centre of the threat was in my own home and revolved around my parents. My mother, although much less overpowering than my father, played her own role. Some years after Dad's death, a family relative described Mother as "long-suffering." I don`t think that description is quite accurate or does her justice. Indeed she was a kind and gentle person but she was neither passive nor resigned. Instead, she faced reality, and the reality was that Dad was a problem drinker and at times a bully. Mother knew this, accepted it and decided to make the best of it. She felt this was what God wanted her to do. Ultimately her actions and indeed her life rested on her faith in a loving God. She found strength and solace in her devotion to the rosary, the Sacred Heart (we always went to mass and communion on the nine first Fridays of the year in honour of the Sacred Heart) and the Communion of Saints. On All Souls' Day, November 2, we spent most of the day at church making visits for her dead relatives and friends who might still need her prayers. My mother's life was grounded in her faith, and if I sometimes resented her failure to intervene against my father's aggression, I now realize that her own serenity derived, in large measure, from accepting in faith the things she could not change.

So Mother's life revolved around her religion, her home and a few friends, although I worried sometimes that we did not have as many friends as other people. Did my parents have a happy marriage? Certainly they both shared deeply their religious faith. They both loved to drive and in 1935 when she was forty-six, Mother won first prize for the best-decorated car in Hastings' Centennial Parade. The parade had been organized by Dad, and it was the biggest and the best in the town's hundred-year history. My parents also shared a keen interest in lawn bowling, often driving home late from district tournaments in places like Havelock (where Mother's younger sister, Geraldine, lived with her family) with Stafford and me asleep in the back of the car. Sometimes they drove with friends to a film in Peterborough, leaving Stafford and me with a baby-sitter or the maid we had for several years. They enjoyed Ginger Rogers and Fred Astaire and never missed a film with Oscar O'Shea of *Captains Courageous* fame because he was the brother of Mona, our dearest family cousin. I think Dad's favourite films were *Birth of a Nation* and *All Quiet on the Western Front*. Mother played the piano and insisted for years that I take lessons which I did reluctantly and then dropped. Dad, basically a self-educated man, read some history and biography.

On Wednesday afternoons, a half-holiday for the stores in Hastings, Dad would come home for the noon meal as usual. Then he and Mother would go upstairs for a rest. One Wednesday afternoon I burst into their bedroom to ask for something or other. Mother, lying on the bed half naked, looked startled and pulled the sheets up over her breasts. Dad swerved round and angrily ordered me out of the room. I never made that mistake again. It was the closest I ever came to a glimpse of my parents' sex life.

And yet, despite what they had in common, I wonder how well my parents communicated with each other and with Stafford and me. Dad's alcoholism was an open sore filling our house with its bitter stench. Yet I never knew our parents to discuss this with each other or with us. For that matter, although my father's drinking soured my growing up, I never raised it with him or my mother. As with similar problems in other families of that era, it was swept under the rug. This lack of honest communication in our house made the atmosphere confusing and threatening. I would hear from someone else what Dad thought of my school. I would hear two farmers who were waiting beside the wicket at the bank laughing and joking about my father's boozing. And still Dad would sometimes say one thing and do another. Long after my friends were going to the Friday night dances at Lynch's

Hall, I was not permitted to go. But when a new dance pavilion opened on the hill overlooking the Trent River, my parents were there - in spite of the fact that Father Garvey had warned that the pavilion would be a cesspool of sins, most of them sexual and all of them mortal.

Every now and then I would fight back out of rage and resentment against a discipline that I considered unfair and which was making me feel more different than ever from my peers. One night at supper, disgusted with Dad's reeking of alcohol and his badgering me about some shortcoming, I exploded and I did what I had never dared do before - I threatened him with exposure. I told him I was going to see the parish priest and tell him everything. I'm not sure now what I was going to tell and I suspect a good part of the threat was bluff. The other part involved his drinking, his cursing and one other curious phenomenon. The parish priest expected my father to provide all the daily hardware requirements for the church, but when there were major repairs to be done, the priest would go to Peterborough to contract the job. Then Dad would become angry at the Church and say we would be better off as communists - at least they treated everyone the same. I imagine it was some grab bag of similar accusations that formed my vague indictment against my father. Dad tried to reason with me. I sensed his concern, but rejected his attempt at conciliation. Mother was frightened. What was this terrible secret that I was withholding from her husband and why did I want to tell our parish priest? In any event, we never went to see the priest, and the incident blew over. But for whatever it was worth, I felt I had won something, if only my father's attention. Perhaps I even scared him. In some way I had expanded my own autonomy and, even if only briefly, had defeated him. But it was a short-lived victory because presently he made a decision which I would ferociously resent and which would change my life.

3

DEATH AND THE JESUITS

In June 1942, I completed my junior matriculation at Campbellford High and expected to return there for my final year in the all-important Grade Thirteen. However, because of a county dispute about taxes, the school bus to Campbellford stopped running. Some of my friends would go to Norwood High and others planned to board with friends in Campbellford and finish the year there, which is what I hoped to do. But Dad had other plans. Apparently he still thought there was humping going on behind the bushes in Campbellford. He made inquiries and heard from a priest friend about Regiopolis College, a Jesuit boarding school in Kingston, Ontario. He decided to send Stafford and me there.

I knew nothing of the Jesuits and I didn't want to know anything about them. I fought my father with every weapon I had, arguments, threats, tears, ultimatums. Nothing worked. So one Sunday morning in September 1942, Stafford (who wasn't as upset as I was) and I piled into the car with our parents, drove the hundred miles to Kingston and had our first glimpse of the ivy-covered grey limestone buildings. This was Regiopolis College or "Regi" for short. It looked like a prison.

As I unpacked my suitcase outside the top-floor senior dormitory, I felt sick to my stomach. I knew no one in my class. Many of the other boarders and day students had been together for several years. Friendships had been made and cliques formed. If at Campbellford I sometimes felt the outsider, at Regiopolis I would always feel that way. A young Jesuit scholastic-in-training assigned me a space in the senior dormitory with its shining waxed floors and twenty-five beds neatly made up under bright red coverlets. I was uncomfortable showering and sleeping with a group of strangers but I did my best to disguise my feelings. Not long after, I began to have trouble sleeping, a problem which has plagued the rest of my life. Perhaps, in view of the years of stress and strain at home, Regi was the occasion rather than the principal cause of my chronic insomnia.

The year at Regi was the loneliest of my life. I remember the loneliness seeping into my bones like a wet November drizzle soaking the muddy ground between the limestone buildings. I still get the shivers every time I pass through Kingston. But misery loves company and I did make one friend, a chap named Farrell from Belleville, who was as miserable as I was. While other boarders went to the movies on Saturday afternoons, Farrell and I tramped the desolate streets of Kingston commiserating with each other. We were both counting the days until the Thanksgiving holiday. Stafford was in the hospital with chickenpox, but I expected to go home anyway. Imagine my consternation when Dad informed me I was to remain at the school. This information must have come to me in a letter from Mother because Dad never wrote and I do not remember either of my parents telephoning on a regular basis. The message was that the hundred-mile trip home for Thanksgiving was too expensive. Dad once remarked what a financial sacrifice he and Mother were making to send us both to an expensive Jesuit boarding school and I'm sure it was true. Feeling resentful and rejected, I appealed to my mother to intercede with my father. She did, and finally telephoned to say that although Stafford would remain in the hospital, I could come home.

Sometime after Thanksgiving, I moved to another residence called Spratt House where I had a private room, a welcome improvement. I also made a friend among the Jesuits, on the whole an intimidating and remote lot. Father Boyle was my Latin teacher, a chaplain at the penitentiary and eventually a confidante. When I was down in the dumps and the loneliness ached like a rotten tooth, I would go to Father Boyle's room for a chat. He was a friendly man with an ironic sense of humour and invariably he bucked me up. Sometimes we talked about the possibility of my having a vocation to the priesthood, maybe even to the Jesuits.

Father Boyle was always temperate on the subject of vocations. Not so Joe Driscoll, a young Jesuit scholastic teacher from Boston, brash, oozing Irish charm, who had no trouble gathering a coterie of students around him. We often sat around in Spratt House and shot the breeze. But Joe Driscoll, underneath his bubbly personality, had his own agenda, which was to spot likely candidates for the Jesuit order. I am not sure the founder of the order, St. Ignatius of Loyola, would have approved all his methods, but Joe Driscoll was a persuasive recruiter. Many young men in English Canada joined the Jesuits because of Driscoll's spiritual pep talks. I would run into Joe Driscoll again the following year at St. Michael's College in Toronto, where he would give me his undivided attention.

Finally the abysmal year with the Jesuits in Kingston ended when, because of the war, we were let out of school early in the spring of 1943. If our marks were high enough and we worked for thirteen weeks on a farm to help the war effort, we would pass the year automatically. My marks at Regi were reasonably good, especially in English and history, but I was struggling with trigonometry. I spent the thirteen weeks at Joe Gorman's farm outside Hastings coiling hay, milking cows and driving a team of horses. I don't know how much I helped the war effort, but the war enabled me to pass trigonometry.

Sometime in the summer of 1943, my parents decided that I should enroll for a B.A. degree at another prestigious Catholic school, St. Michael's College in Toronto. (Did some priest advise them that this was the best way to test a vocation?) The year at St. Mike's was as different from Regi as a dance floor from a prison cell. At St. Mike's I made several friends and got on well with the Basilian Fathers, who seemed a lot friendlier than the Jesuits. I didn't work too hard at my courses (especially Latin and Greek, both of which I failed), felt part of the gang when we all went down to Spadina Avenue to a strip joint, looked forward to the weekly dances at St. Basil's parish hall, met a girl there whom I began to walk home past the gravestones of St. James's Cemetery and with whom I enjoyed my first French kiss. At St. Mike's I felt a rock had dissolved in my stomach.

No sooner had I arrived home in Hastings after the year at St. Mike's than the old anxiety returned like a storm cloud. As usual, Dad was lying on the living-room couch snoring and sleeping off his day's drinking. But there was something else tonight, something unusual. His face had a slack jaundiced look. I had known vaguely for some time that he was not well. Some months earlier he had gone to Toronto for a medical appointment. I never learned fully or directly what his doctors diagnosed. From ambiguous remarks from Mother and other relatives, I surmised that Dad had terminal cancer. But as with his alcoholism, his illness was swept under the rug and discussed only in whispers behind shielding hands - our family's way of dealing with serious problems, which only raised my level of anxiety and dread. And it is a measure of the level of communication in our house that I am not sure to this day what eventually caused my father's death.

So it was typical on my first night home from St. Mike's, as I was helping Mother dry the supper dishes, that she referred to Dad's condition only in vague terms and asked me not to go out that evening to the dance at Lynch's Hall. Disturbed by this new fear filling the house like a noxious fog, I curtly told Mother that I had to get away and escaped to the gaiety of the dance. So began the summer of 1944 and the last few weeks of my father's life, an anxious, depressing and guilt-ridden time, relieved only by an exciting moment early on the morning of June 6 when I ran upstairs to tell my parents the D-day invasion of Europe was under way, then joyfully moved the miniature flags on the war map I had kept on the kitchen wall since the fall of 1939.

One day later that summer I was standing alone with Dad in the hardware store. He was dressed in his best blue suit and tie. This was unusual for him because he was basically a working man, at home on a farmer's roof repairing the eaves trough with his soldering iron and blow torch, or looking forward to a farming dinner of salt pork, mashed potatoes and gravy. I was standing beside the bundles of binder twine when he turned to me and spoke in a tone of voice I had seldom heard before, soft and gentle. He said nothing directly about his illness. Instead he remarked quietly, as if he had thought about his words for a long time, that he might not be there for long and I would have to look after Mother and the store. I now know it was his way of telling me he was going to die, his way of asking me for help. To my shame, his words simply made me uneasy and uncomfortable. Dad was trying to reach an emotional terrain we had never traversed. I had no response because I had no map. I was lost. I just turned away.

During most of July, Dad spent a good deal of time in bed on the upstairs screened-in porch overlooking the Anglican church, Foulds' barns and our neighbours' houses on Bridge Street. He prayed often to the Blessed Virgin and to the North American Jesuit Martyrs, Brébeuf and Lalement and their companions, to whom he had long had a special devotion. He became tranquil and serene in a way I had never seen before. Still I felt fear and guilt during the days of his dying. One night he fell out of bed and Mother had to summon a neighbour to help her. Both Stafford and I found it suffocating to stay around the house. At the same time I felt guilty about leaving Mother alone. Finally, on the morning of August 4, in his sixty-second year, after receiving all the sacramental rites of the Church, my father died. I was kneeling at the end of his bed.

Now, much later, I try to remember the good things about my father. He was an honest man respected in his community, a good provider, self-educated, a man of genuine faith. He was a generous man. Running a store in the Depression, he carried on his books the accounts of many customers when they couldn't afford to pay, and in some cases he cancelled their debts entirely. He was enterprising, even creative. One night the doctor summoned him in the middle of the night to cut a fishhook out of a man's eye. Dad maneuvered his tinsmith tools and did the job safely.

He liked simple pleasures such as holiday drives to Stony Lake. There Mother would prepare a picnic on the flat rocks beside the water and cook hamburgers and hot dogs on the little galvanized picnic stove Dad had made in the tinsmith shop. He always cooked our Sunday dinner and served it piping hot, a quality he rigorously required for all our meals. Dad was a sports fan and invested his own money in the local ball team. He often went to games, where he would sit in the same seat - which had his name carved in it - and loudly heckle the umpire, usually Bill Wellman, the Hastings police chief, who had a habit of turning his head and spewing a stream of tobacco juice between pitches. In the fall Dad always took a radio to the store for the baseball world series. He was an avid fan of the New York Yankees when they had their celebrated Murderers' Row anchored by Lou Gehrig and Babe Ruth.

Dad had a sense of humour - never more so than when it came to politics. He discussed politics both at the store with his customers and at home with Grandfather Shea and Uncle Dan. Like most Catholics, he was a red-hot Liberal and always supported Mackenzie King. He had great fun during the federal election campaign of

1940 when he pointed out to his Orangemen friends, most of them Conservatives, that he couldn't lose no matter what happened. Either King (a Liberal) would win again or Robert Manion (a Roman Catholic) would win. Either way Dad could claim victory.

Naturally, Dad was proud of his store and his successful record in business. At the back of the store, outside the cellar, flowed a raceway from the river. One night someone in a boat broke into the cellar and robbed the store. The village poet and bootlegger, Al Scriver, commemorated the break-in and the store in *The Hastings Star* this way:

> I know a man of great renown,
> He keeps a store in our town.
> A man who each and all know well,
> In hardware lives he does excel.
> I met this man and was I shocked
> To hear him say, "I'm over-stocked.
> And anyone with a canoe,
> Here's all these folks now have to do:
> Just paddle up to my back door,
> Walk up the steps into the store,
> Then look around and help yourself
> To anything that's on the shelf.
> You'll find I have a fine collection
> Of hardware goods for your selection.
> There's varnishes and paints and oils,
> Roasting pans and wire coils,
> Nuts and bolts and locks and clasps,
> Hatchets, ratchets, wrenches, rasps,
> Hammers, axes, saws and files,
> And rope enough to reach ten miles.
> Brushes, brooms, and mops and nails,
> Boilers, washtubs, water pails,
> Knives and forks, all kinds of delf,
> Are piled up there upon the shelf.
> Cages for all kinds of pets,
> Bamboo poles and landing nets,
> Stoves that burn both coal and oil,
> Fertilizer for the soil,

Kiddie cars for kids to ride,
Pots with handles on the side,
All kinds of bait for catching fish,
Most anything that one could wish.
Tonic for your swine and chicks,
Shovels, crowbars, forks and picks,
Mowers for to mow your grass,
Points for ploughs, and window glass,
Traps for rats, and traps for mice,
Carving knives your meat to slice.
And right there by the east partition,
You'll find my stock of ammunition.
This may sound good but better still,
I'll leave some money in the till.
So use your boat, till I decide
To leave my front door open wide.
Take everything both large and small,
Just leave the store for me, that's all.
Yes, help yourself for I have plenty.
What's mine is yours, A.J. McKenty."

Dad was astounded to read Al Scriver's list of merchandise. He said Al had listed items he never knew he had. And one night he almost lost them all. It was on August 1, 1940. Mother was in Hanover helping her sister Geraldine, who was dying of cancer. Shortly after one o'clock in the morning, fire swept through two buildings on Main Street, threatening the store. The police called him and he roused me from a deep sleep. The night of the big fire was doubly important for me because Dad, alert and sober, confided in me that he thought we would lose the store and we would just have to carry on somehow for Mother and Stafford's sake. He was not overly upset and I felt he was treating me as an ally, that he needed my support, that both of us, my father and I, were in this crisis together. It was a feeling of closeness and camaraderie that I had not experienced before and seldom would again. I don't know why this window opened so briefly and then closed again. Nor do I know why, when Dad offered to stock the side window of the store for Stafford and me and let us have the profits in lieu of an allowance, we both rejected the offer.

43

What I don't know about my father was the source of his pain - perhaps the early loss of his parents or the war which he refused to talk about. I do know he was a good man.

4

WHIPS AND CHAINS

My father's death delayed plans I had made while at St. Michael's College. With the war on - and Dad's advice to stay out of it - I worried a lot about what to do with my life. First, I thought of becoming a lawyer, influenced perhaps by the newspaper and radio accounts of the Lindbergh baby's kidnapping. I avidly followed the trial, conviction and execution of Bruno Hauptmann. As often as I could, I would take the bus to Peterborough and spend the day in the courthouse, seeing a variety of trials. Even now, whenever I am in London, I visit the Old Bailey criminal courts to attend a murder trial.

In addition to the law, I had developed another interest early on - journalism, both print and radio. Naturally my writing for *The Peterborough Examiner* as a teenager stimulated my enthusiasm for a reporting career. But I was just as fascinated by broadcast journalism. For a long time my parents thought a radio was too mundane so Stafford and I had to visit a neighbour to listen to the annual broadcast of the Santa Claus parade. When we were finally allowed to have a radio, I remember listening to the Democratic Convention of 1940 where Franklin Roosevelt was nominated for an unprecedented third term. I never missed the staccato news delivery of Walter Winchell bombarding "Mr. and Mrs. North America and all the ships at sea." And Sunday night, after everyone else had gone to bed, I would remain downstairs reading aloud Walter Winchell's weekly column, trying to imitate his machine-gun delivery, until Dad would roar down for me to shut up. He often did the same thing when I was playing games in the back yard, accusing me of being too bossy and too loud, accusations that had considerable validity.

One day while still in high school, after an especially bitter argument with Dad, I decided to run away from home - somewhat of an exaggeration since I took the bus to Peterborough after breakfast and returned on the same bus in time for supper. I expect this was yet another attempt to escape my father's authority and it involved considerable initiative of my own, because, while in Peterborough, I managed to talk my way into radio station CHEX and convince the program director to give me an audition - which he did by asking me to read cold in front of a microphone a few news items from *The Examiner*. Then he told me to finish high school, obtain my parents' permission and keep up my interest in radio. I did, but it would be more than thirty years before anything came of it.

By the spring of 1944, however, I had made a decision that ruled out both law and journalism. I had decided I wanted to become a Jesuit priest. This may seem a curious choice, considering the miserable year I had had with the Jesuits in Kingston. But now, many years later, I can try to disentangle the confusing strands that comprised this decision. As a youngster and as an altar boy, I had frequently heard of the honour associated with the priesthood. I knew several priests well and frequently heard them talk or preach about vocations. Some people in the parish told me that they expected me to become a priest. So, I thought, did Mother. Dad kept his thoughts to himself. And somewhere along the line I inferred that God might be calling me to be a priest - all the more probable because my best friend, Tim Coughlan, had been accepted into the seminary.

Tim Coughlan, a year younger than I, was no Goody Two-shoes, but he had solid values and a genuine sense of humour. He enjoyed life and wasn't above a little innocent fun. We scared the hell out of a friend's cows one time when we tried to milk them, and we scared our two elementary school teachers by following them at a safe distance through the woods - and were later found out and punished for it. Tim and I played hockey and other sports together and barely missed blowing off our toes when shooting groundhogs. I think what I really appreciated about Tim Coughlan was how normal he was.

This was the position - a definite attraction combined with a worrisome uncertainty - with which I had begun the previous year at St. Mike's. Then my erstwhile friend from Regiopolos days, Joe Driscoll of the Society of Jesus, self-appointed Jesuit recruiter, reappeared on the scene. Driscoll was then in Toronto at the seminary preparing for his ordination to the priesthood. Early in the fall of 1943, he contacted me by telephone. From then on, most Thursday afternoons Driscoll and I tramped the streets of Toronto talking a mile a minute. Always, a good part of the time was devoted to the question of my having a vocation to the priesthood and more specifically to the Jesuits. So, after innumerable discussions with Joe Driscoll on the subject, I gradually drifted toward two conclusions: God was probably calling me to the priesthood, and if I was going to become a priest I might as well be the best, a Jesuit. Many years later I would change my view on the first part of that proposition, but despite all that has happened in the interval, I have never changed my opinion on the second. There was another circumstantial reason favouring the Jesuits. Seven or eight of my fellow Regi students, including Edgar Burns whom I had come to admire a great deal, had joined the Jesuits or were about to.

So I applied to the English-speaking Canadian province of the Jesuits, filled out a lot of papers, had an interview with the Jesuit provincial who lived in an impressive house in Toronto's wealthy Rosedale district, and was accepted to enter the Jesuit novitiate at Guelph on July 31 - the feast day of the founder of the Jesuit order, Ignatius of Loyola, a Spanish priest who had once been a soldier.

Because of Dad's illness and death, the date for entering the novitiate was postponed until September 8, and there was some discussion of postponing it indefinitely. A priest friend of our family told me my first obligation was to remain home to help my newly-widowed mother with her affairs, especially the running of the hardware store. In addition to Dad's death, two factors made the situation at the store precarious. It had been moved to a less satisfactory location because of a dispute about the lease - which had clouded Dad's last months. Also, my father's able assistant of many years, Ray Boyle, was drafted into the army. So at the age of seventeen, Stafford, who had dropped out of Regi, was running the hardware store.

Stafford, called Sam by his friends, was two years younger than I, and strange and sad to say, we never developed a close relationship. He had his own friends and seemed to me more sociable than I was. Now I'm not so sure. He often said I was like our mother and he was like our dad. Certainly, Staff was laconic, reserved, dismissive of anything intellectual, although he was bright enough in subjects like mathematics and science.

We had little in common and that little was sabotaged by the difference in our personalities. I was domineering and Stafford was stubborn. It seems incredible to me now, but I think I sometimes treated my brother the way our father treated me. I tried to bully Staff. I remember one night when we were both still very young and sleeping a foot apart in our bedroom. I drew a verbal picture of damnation and hellfire for him, not unlike the religious terrorism of the Redemptorists, which frightened him so much he began to cry. But usually Staff didn't cry at my strictures. He either fought back or ignored them. So our relationship was warped from the beginning.

I don't know what Stafford's feelings were when he had to take over the store. We never confided in each other. He had shown some interest in Dad's trade, tinsmithing, but had not developed any special skills. What he had developed and what was quickly complicating our relationship further was a drinking problem. By the time I was preparing to leave for Guelph, both Mother and I realized that Staff's drinking was becoming dangerous, but like all the problems in our house, little was said about it. Just before I left Hastings, I took Stafford into our back yard and tried to warn him about his drinking. He denied there was a problem, looked sullen and resentful and simply refused to discuss it.

This convinced me that Staff and I would never be able to run the store amicably. I was also concerned about my status with the army, and I think I just wanted to escape all the anxiety and discomfort my home had represented for so long. Mother, worried as I am certain she was about the store and Staff's drinking, did not press me to stay - far from it. I am sure she saw my course as a manifestation of God's will which she accepted generously. I was less generous. The night before I left, Mother and I were in my bedroom packing my suitcases and talking. Suddenly I snapped at her that I was going, and that was that. Undoubtedly the upset occurred because of my own feelings of ambiguity and guilt about the course upon which I was embarking.

So on Saturday night at ten o'clock, September 5, 1944, I locked the doors of Dad's hardware store for the last time and walked to a cottage beyond the locks of the Trent River. Staying at the cottage was a girl visiting from Toronto. We rolled around on the bed and did some necking. This provoked more feelings of guilt. How could God be calling me to be a priest while I was physically groping around with a casual friend whom I would never see again? And with time running out, where would I get rid of this guilt in confession? This was not a happy prelude to my life in the Society of Jesus.

Somehow or other, being in the state of mortal sin - all sexual sins were mortal - on Sunday morning I managed to avoid going up for holy communion at my last mass in Our Lady of Mount Carmel parish where I had spent so many years as the head altar boy. Next morning Mother and I caught the early train for Peterborough and Toronto and, since Jesuits did not normally return home, I gazed outside the window watching the mist rise over the river like a silken tablecloth and wondered if I would ever see Hastings again. In Toronto, where we were staying with friends, I had to find a priest who would hear my confession so I would not begin my Jesuit life in a state of mortal sin. Fortunately I found one before mass on Tuesday morning, and left the confessional box with that sudden rush of relief, realizing my sweaty and sinful guilt had evaporated yet again.

The highlight of our Toronto visit was going to Massey Hall to hear the famous Catholic orator, Monsignor Fulton Sheen. He had been a hero of mine since we first listened to his radio talks in the thirties. Later, Monsignor Sheen became even more famous when his television program had higher ratings than that of the comedian Milton Berle. To the sound of music, Fulton Sheen swept onto the stage of Massey Hall, his bright red cape shimmering in the lights, his blue eyes piercing, his smile radiant. As his voice soared, I soared too. Fulton Sheen was a priest. I was going to be a priest. Maybe I would be as famous a priest as he.

Some of this elation had dribbled away by the time Mother and I reached Guelph at noon the next day. Over lunch in a dreary restaurant we felt uneasy, our conversation forced. Then the moment arrived. We called a cab and asked to be driven to the Jesuit novitiate on the outskirts of Guelph. Just beyond the road to Kitchener, we came to a long fence backed by clipped green bushes and manicured lawns. Behind the fence we could see a plaque that read, "Rest in Peace, All Ye Who Enter Here." That sounded about right, so we told our cab driver to "Go in here." Unfortunately, this impressive spread turned out to be the Catholic cemetery. Trying to hide our embarrassment, we watched the driver turn around and drive back out, meanwhile snatching what "peace" we could.

The novitiate was up the next road, a long lane lined by maple trees. We emerged onto a green lawn spangled with bright red and white circular flower beds before an impressive portico on two white columns which fronted a large white and grey house, a typical nineteenth-century country estate. A young novice invited Mother and me into the gleaming visitors' parlour - everything gleamed in the novitiate with its faint aroma of fresh wax - where we were to meet the master of novices, Father Brendan Cloran, S.J. In some respects, a novice master in the Jesuits corresponds to a commandant in the Marines. He runs the program, lock, stock and barrel, twenty-four hours a day, seven days a week. His authority is absolute because he stands in the place of Christ as far as obedience is concerned - no ifs, ands or buts.

Father Cloran came into the parlour to welcome us. In spite of the tailored black Jesuit cassock neatly cinctured at the waist, he looked like a successful middle manager from the world we had just left. He was just under six feet tall, trim and well set up, with a ruddy face that looked freshly shaved. He had an expression that flitted between neutral friendly and slightly stern and a laugh that was carefully controlled, as was much else about Father Cloran. Later, I would see that his gait and body language as he walked briskly along the outside balconies saying his daily office was always purposeful. He had little use for chitchat or small talk. I heard later that Father Cloran often exhibited an engaging sense of humour with his Jesuit peers. But I would detect little evidence of that in the 750 or so days I was to spend under his tutelage in the novitiate. His whole manner was brisk rather than brusque. Any lonely novice looking for sympathy would be disappointed. In a word, Brendan Cloran was a straight-shooter. On this first occasion, he remained only long enough to welcome my mother and me. Then he was gone, this man who would dominate every waking hour of my life, and some sleeping ones, for the next two years.

The Jesuits, with their reputation for intellectual prowess and casuistry, were often described as the Pope's light infantry, bright and flexible enough to handle any crisis in the Catholic Church. On the other hand, they were often criticized for following and promoting a spiritual regimen that was too militaristic and mechanical. (In fact, I would one day be interviewed for a documentary with the National Film Board, comparing the Jesuit novitiate to a Marine boot camp.) I should point out that the religious training I am describing here took place in Canada, in one Jesuit novitiate, in 1944. Doubtless there have been many changes and modifications since, including the use of sophisticated psychological tests to determine the suitability of candidates to enter and continue in the novitiate.

The four elements that made up novitiate life involved prayer, penance, work, and recreation. We were introduced to Jesuit prayer intensively at the start of the long retreat which began at the end of September and lasted a month. The long retreat involved a series of daily spiritual exercises which had been constructed by St. Ignatius. These exhibited a psychological acumen far ahead of his time. The exercises were an intensive and compressed experience of Ignatian spirituality. With the exception of four "break days," the retreat was made in silence. The schedule pivoted on four meditations a day. This meant the master of novices gave a half-hour talk, usually based upon passages from scripture. Then all eight of us trooped into our prayer and reading room called the ascetory where we each knelt on our prie-dieu beside our small wooden desk, and meditated on what the master had said. After fifty minutes we wrote down in a small book any "lights" we had received during our meditation period.

I must confess the pages of my "lights" book remained largely blank and the entries were rather forced and dim. Thirty days of intensive spiritual exercises for young men who have just emerged from Winnipeg or Toronto or Montreal or even Hastings is a long time. It was made longer by the master's approach. This was Father Cloran's first year as master of novices. So far as I know, he had had no special training for the position; he certainly had no special flair for dealing with young men. His obvious sincerity did not compensate for his lack of spiritual and psychological insight. His presentations, four times a day, were generally uninspired and uninspiring. His personal spiritual direction did not seem to get much beyond the last book he had read. This first long retreat was a little like trudging through deep snow with neither skis nor snowshoes nor an adequate guide. Two daily periods of meditation continued for the rest of the novitiate training; we rose to the clanging of morning bells at 5:30, meditated an hour before breakfast from six to seven, then meditated another half hour in the evening before supper.

Hand in glove with our practice of prayer went our discipline of penance, not just the familiar penance of fasting which we had done at home in Hastings on Fridays and during Lent, but a penance more dramatic and more troublesome. This included two innocent looking instruments, the one a foot-long whip of braided white cords, the other a bracelet of thin chains, their sharpened points facing inwards. A couple of nights a week in the dormitory, each novice drew the curtains around his bed, removed his clothes and rummaged around in his bureau for his whip. At the sound of a bell, rung by the senior novice called the admonitor, the lights were flicked off and in the darkness each novice whipped, or more accurately flagellated, himself for the space of an Our Father, when the lights would come on again.

Some of the less fervent novices were suspected of flagellating themselves with their cassocks still on. This hurt less but made more noise. The admonition from the master on this flagellation was clear. We could whip ourselves as hard as we liked so long as we did not draw blood. The same warning applied to the steel bracelet. It was worn a few mornings a week from rising until after breakfast, snapped tightly around the ankle or arm but not so tightly as to break the skin and cause bleeding. One morning as one novice was walking up the centre aisle of the chapel for mass, the chain fell from his ankle onto the floor. We all realized he had been in no danger of drawing blood.

These mediaeval penitential practices did no physical damage. To what extent they did psychological harm is another question. If nothing else, they intensified the already tense atmosphere in the novitiate. From morning until night the novice was urged in all his actions to strive to live the Jesuit motto, *Ad Majorem Dei Gloriam*, For the Greater Glory of God. Not only was this motto preached incessantly, but the Jesuit models who had lived it were held up for our edification, especially the boy saints like John Berchmans and Aloysius Gonzaga. Saint John Berchmans lived in the seventeenth century, an apple-cheeked Belgian boy who died in the novitiate, possibly before he reached puberty. Saint Aloysius Gonzaga, from an illustrious Italian family, refused to look at his mother's face after he took the vow of chastity.

But even if we could emulate Berchmans and Gonzaga without going to the infirmary for a tranquilizer (which would be refused), what about that other paragon of penitential practice, the Irish Jesuit who lived early in this century, the eccentric Willie Doyle? Father Willie Doyle of the Society of Jesus was famous for standing half the night in icy Irish bogs with his arms held out in the form of a cross. He whipped himself until his blood ran down and soaked into the ground. He wore piercing brambles and chains all over his body until his skin was as full of holes as a dart board. I have no doubt that Father Willie Doyle cut himself to ribbons for the greater glory of God as he understood it. I do wonder why a book extolling these practices was in the novitiate library, along with others of the same ilk, available to all the impressionable novices for their study and edification.

These practices merely heightened the novitiate climate, which often resembled that of a steamy greenhouse. The maze of rules, regulations, traditions, and bells to stop this and start that (ringing thirty or forty times between our rising at 5:30 and lights-out at 9:30) was bound to produce a jumpy atmosphere in which one's nervous system itself became jittery. Novices who became too tense were sent to the barn to work out their stress pitching hay. One rule stipulated if we were ordered to stop what we were doing, even if we were writing a letter home, then we must stop immediately. One would likely interpret that to mean we should stop at the end of the word we were writing. Not so. Stopping your letter meant that if you were writing the letter "s" you should stop in the middle of it.

All conversations in the ascetory were carried on in Latin which some of us spoke about as well as Swahili. And twenty novices living in close proximity twenty-four hours a day inevitably resulted in irritations and aggravations, small enough but often magnified out of all proportion. I remember a fellow novice who laughed loud and laughed often. At some point I concluded his laugh was artificial and phony. It wasn't far from that to judge that he also was artificial and phony and was driving me bonkers. Naturally, this attitude clashed head on with the virtue of charity which we were supposed to be practising day and night. I was to love my laughing fellow novice like a brother. This dilemma set up an interior tension that I was never able to resolve satisfactorily until the poor chap (who knew nothing of my feelings for him) left the novitiate for good. I must admit I found his departure a relief.

Not only were we living in an emotional hothouse, we were also living under a magnifying glass, in that actions and reactions were distorted and dilated out of all proportion. For example, on our weekly Thursday holiday, instead of porridge for breakfast we would have dry cereal. A favourite pastime of some novices out for a walk after supper on Wednesday night was to peer through the refectory windows to make certain the cereal boxes were actually on the tables - and this at a time when other Canadian twenty-year olds were fighting their way across Europe toward the Rhine.

Or take the tradition of "angels." When a new novice candidate entered, the master would appoint an angel to stick to the novice like a leech to show him the ropes for a two-week period called postulancy. To be chosen an angel was considered a feather in one's cap, and there was a lot of underground speculation about whom the master would choose. Sometimes those not chosen would go into a funk. Were they not worthy? Maybe the master didn't like them. For some reason, I was chosen as an angel in my first year.

The appointment of the admonitor was an even more important event. The admonitor, always a second-year novice, was the master's eyes and ears on his flock. The admonitor reported daily to the master, put up notices, saw to it that rules were obeyed, consulted the diary in which novitiate traditions were inscribed, assigned the work, named "bands" (who was to walk with whom during recreation), and presided from a corner in the ascetory nearest to the master's room upstairs. The master, who scarcely ever came into the ascetory, would choose the admonitor for a period of three or four months. There was as much speculation about the selection of a new admonitor as there would be about the choice of a leader for a political party. Sometimes the appointment of a new admonitor provoked fear, sometimes relief, sometimes jealousy. This was natural enough. Was it also natural how turbulently these emotions flowed underneath the placid façade of holy charity?

In the program there were two elements designed to give a measure of relief from the intensity of novitiate life. These were work and recreation. Work involved everything from cleaning toilets to driving a team of horses. The novitiate was the hub of a thriving farm of several hundred acres supporting dairy cows, grain crops, honey bees, and extensive apple orchards. In fact, the orchards were so outstanding they were studied by students from the Ontario Agricultural College, which was on the other side of Guelph. The farm and the orchards were run by the lay brothers, sometimes called coadjutor brothers, Jesuits who took perpetual vows but were not ordained priests. Eventually I came to admire some of these brothers as the most impressive and solid Jesuits in the entire English-Canadian province. They gave much, asked little and had their spiritual boots, often muddy, planted solidly on the ground. We had the good fortune to work with them, especially in the late summer and fall bringing in the crops and picking apples.

Most of our work assignments were more pedestrian: setting and cleaning refectory tables; washing dishes after meals; polishing wood; cleaning bathrooms; scrubbing toilets; looking after the altars, the sanctuary and the sacristy; and sometimes helping sick or elderly Jesuits who lived in the house. No doubt this physical activity was nourishing for our health and restraining for our libido. I never believed the canard that saltpetre was sprinkled in our food.

Our daily recreation occurred after the noon dinner and the evening supper, meals that were substantial, healthy and dull. Conversation during the first part of ordinary recreation was in French or Latin, and since I was not fluent in either language, I kept reasonably silent until the admonitor shouted that we could speak English. We usually walked in bands of three assigned by the admonitor. Sometimes the other members in my band were adept in French or Latin or both. These were usually the Jesuit novices who had gone through the entire school system at Loyola in Montreal. With them I tried not to feel inferior, gritted my teeth and did my best. Trying to speak Latin in a howling blizzard, the temperature twenty below zero, to two people I didn't especially like, was not my idea of recreation then nor is it now.

Thursday after breakfast until meditation before supper was still our holiday, as it was in most Jesuit houses the world over. We played softball on the lower meadow beyond the beehives and went for long walks, always in groups of three decided by the admonitor, along the picturesque roads around Guelph and the Puslinch area (where we also taught catechism in some of the Catholic schools). About a mile from the novitiate house, across the road and through a light wood on the banks of the Speed River, we had what was euphemistically called a villa. It was actually an old clapboard house in considerable disrepair. Nonetheless, here we had a good deal of fun, including swimming and boisterous treasure hunts. Late one afternoon in April 1945, walking back through the wet spring fields after a happy day at the villa, we heard the sad news that President Roosevelt had died.

Sometime in the second year of my novitiate, speculation began about whether the master would appoint me admonitor. Naturally I began to fantasize about the possibility. Such fantasies contain their own spiritual traps. On the one hand, humility required that I not seek advancement of any kind. On the other hand, I badly needed some sign of reassurance from the master. Part of my problem was my insomnia. It had become worse and was making my days miserable. Lying awake at night, rising at 5:30 and facing a day filled with bells and spiritual potholes was not a formula for peace within myself or for generosity towards others. I tried to cope with the insomnia by saying it was God's will for me at the time, because when I spoke about it with the master he had no other suggestions.

My chronic insomnia was accompanied by persistent anxiety about whether I should be in the novitiate at all, an anxiety that waxed and waned like a persistent headache. Mother, who wrote me long, optimistic letters, occasionally came to visit. Her visits were very uncomfortable for me although I tried to disguise it. She never complained. She was proud her son was in training to become a Jesuit priest, which may have been part of my discomfort. But she was looking older and I knew the situation in the hardware store was becoming more worrisome as was Stafford's drinking. I remember one day after my mother left, speaking to Edgar Burns, a solid mature novice from Montreal whom I had known at Regiopolos. I spoke of my doubts about my vocation and asked him whether he ever had these doubts. He said no.

So there was considerable relief and reassurance when the master called me to his office bedroom one afternoon and said that he was naming me the new admonitor. I accepted this as a vote of confidence in me and my vocation. I determined to be an outstanding admonitor of whom the master would be proud. Whether my fellow novices liked me or not did not matter so much as the master's selecting me. I interpreted this as a sign that God was selecting me, too.

As admonitor, I saw myself as God's instrument. I was there to make sure that everyone lived the rules as perfectly as possible. Unless other novices spoke Latin when they came to my desk, I wouldn't answer them. When I assigned bands for recreation, I put people together who didn't like each other, presumably in the belief that if they didn't enjoy the walk, I was giving them the opportunity to grow in charity.

Those are just two examples of my program to advance the perfection of the other novices. There were many others. The nadir of my efforts occurred when word spread that I was undertaking a review of the diary, the novitiate rule book, with a view to tightening, perhaps even expanding its regulations. This was the last straw for my fellow novices, even the novices who had once supported me. I now wonder, what in God's name was I trying to do? Was I projecting my own miseries on them by trying to force them into a spiritual procrustean bed they didn't want and suspected was unhealthy? The rebellion occurred when some senior novices - I never discovered who they were - went to the master. As a result, he summoned me to his room and announced that he was removing me from office several weeks earlier than usual. It was a dreadful blow, but under the circumstances it was the only sensible action for him to take. Somehow to disguise my own anxiety and fears, I had assumed a position of rigid control - which was intensely irritating to my fellow novices and extremely destructive to myself.

5

THE THIRD DEGREE

A two-week trip to the shrine of the Jesuit Martyrs at Midland, Ontario, helped take my mind off losing the admonitor's position. The drive itself was remarkable only for the speculation about whether the master would go by way of Toronto. He didn't. This phenomenon reveals another aspect of early Jesuit training - the mania for secrecy. What our next task was, whom we walked with, changes in the schedule - all were concealed until the last minute.

The apogee of this practice of secrecy occurred when a novice left voluntarily or was dismissed. It was as if the novice, with whom we had been living in intimate quarters for maybe a year or so, was suddenly dead and buried. The master never referred to him again. No one explained why he left. And the remaining novices rarely, if ever, spoke his name and then only in whispers. We often wondered about what seemed, on the face of it, an uncharitable attitude toward those who left. Was it because they were considered disloyal to the Society of Jesus? Or was it because any talk about those who jumped over the wall might infect the rest of us, particularly those like myself, who were wavering anyway?

Whatever the reason, the two-week trip to the Martyrs' Shrine was a welcome relief from the rigours of the novitiate. If anything, the second year was more intense than the first, partly, it seems to me, because the spiritual practices became increasingly counter-productive. Take the famous Ignatian examination of conscience (the *Examen*) which was practised twice a day for fifteen minutes before noon and again in the evening. As we each kneeled on our prie-dieu, we did an inventory of the virtue we were working on at the time - charity, humility, modesty of the eyes - and wrote the results in a little lined examen booklet. The problem with this exercise (as indeed with the hour of meditation at six o'clock in the morning) was that it made us more introspective, not more prayerful.

There was another aspect of the examination of conscience even more difficult to justify. Certainly it was not prayer, whatever else it was. A couple of times a week at the noon examen, the admonitor would stop beside the prie-dieu of each kneeling novice. If he so desired, the novice would whisper into the admonitor's ear the perceived fault or faults of another novice. The admonitor then glided across the polished ascetory floor and told the second novice what his anonymous confrere had accused him of. It is fair to speculate that the second novice then spent the remainder of his prayer time trying to determine the identity of the creep who had fingered him. It was a practice more conducive to paranoia than to prayer.

Periodically the mid-morning hour in which the master discoursed in a literalist fashion on the Jesuit rule was replaced by another exercise called the chapter. This meant that a novice knelt in the middle of the floor while his confreres were invited to point out his faults. Some got off easy, some not. On more than one occasion the master intervened to moderate the barbs, perhaps long stored up, that he warned were offensive to charity. There was still another form of penance, this time in the refectory before the noon meal. If you felt so inclined (or more accurately, if God was moving you), you could kneel down in front of the rector's table, kiss the floor, hold out your arms in the form of a cross and before the assembled community confess some fault or other.

The problem with many of these practices was to discern whether, in fact, God was inspiring you or whether you were just into some kind of morbid religious exhibitionism. The discerning of these spirits, good and bad, was one of the most subtle and sophisticated components of the Spiritual Exercises. In my own view, the master did not deal adequately with this fundamental element of Ignatian spirituality. But also to be fair, it should be said that the Exercises had been mutilated and coarsened by decades, if not a century, of religious fundamentalism so prevalent among groups such as the Jansenists. The Exercises that I followed had been buried under layers of legalisms and harshness that too often masked the heart of the Spiritual Exercises - the primacy of love. It is gratifying and somewhat ironic to know that much of the work

60

done to rescue the Exercises from the underbrush of narrow puritanism has been done at Loyola House, the internationally renowned Ignatian Centre of Spirituality at Guelph, the site of my old novitiate.

In the mid-1940s however, our novice master, Father Cloran, worked as best he could with what he had. As a result, the emphasis in the novitiate, for me, was not on discernment and love but on discipline and obedience. Instead of being a liberating experience, much of the novitiate was a constricting one. Rather than being attracted to God, I was driven more deeply into myself. The intensive hothouse spiritual program simply aggravated the illness I had brought into the novitiate. Others who entered the novitiate at the same time with more maturity and a healthier motivation, obviously had a different experience. Some of them have been productive Jesuits for more than half a century.

After we returned from our trip to the Martyrs' Shrine it was time to prepare seriously for the perpetual vows of poverty, chastity and obedience. We would pronounce these vows at the culmination of our two-year novitiate training. The vow of poverty was not a problem for most Jesuits. Essentially, Jesuit poverty was a poverty of dependence which means simply if we needed something we asked for it. If our superior agreed we needed it and had the wherewithal to provide it, he gave it to us. This applied to everything from a toothbrush to a car. In my experience, Jesuit superiors, if anything, erred on the side of generosity.

The vow of chastity was quite another matter. Simply put, deliberately enjoying sex in thought, word or deed was a violation of the vow. For years, impulses to sex had infected me like doses of the flu, but despite running around to find kindly priests to hear my confessions, I never discovered any religious antibiotics to bring my sexual temperature down for any length of time. When it came to imagining fondling a woman's breasts or thinking about the Immaculate Conception, usually it was no contest.

During our spiritual exercises, conferences and retreats, the master of novices stressed absolute purity in matters sexual. Examples of Jesuit saints who whipped themselves into a lather to maintain their chastity were put before us. So were some more practical safeguards such as modesty of the eyes. This meant we kept our eyes cast down on a spot on the ground about three feet in front of our shoes. If our eyes were on the ground, presumably they would be less likely to dwell on the seductive swell of a nun's, or anybody else's, bosom. The view that this practice of modesty of the eyes might lead to an obsession with breasts and other erogenous parts of a woman's anatomy was never addressed.

The second safeguard against the ravages of sex was called the rule of touch, *Noli me tangere,* or more familiarly, Rule 32. It prohibited one Jesuit from touching another Jesuit, even in jest. The rule was simple enough; the assumptions behind it were not. Homosexuality was much more in the closet in 1945 than now. I knew little if anything about it. However, looking back, I doubt there were many homosexuals in our group in the novitiate and certainly no active ones. Instead there were several young men attractive physically and also sexually. The blunt fact of the matter is that the sexual dynamics in a Jesuit novitiate are not that far removed from the sexual dynamics in a federal prison, thus, *Noli me tangere.* Among other things it was meant to discourage Particular Friendships, more familiarly known as P.F.s.

A particular friendship developed when the relationship between two novices who liked each other became overly emotional and too exclusive - another reason for always walking and recreating in threes. These were, in my opinion, friendships of an intense emotional nature perhaps tinged with eroticism. It is not surprising that particular friendships of this nature sprouted in our hothouse atmosphere, and were heightened by loneliness. If these P.F.s were ever expressed physically, I was not aware of it. No matter, when noticed they were not tolerated. Sooner or later, word of the affair would get to the master, and the two friends in question, immersed in their own emotional anguish, would be called separately to his office. The relationship would then end or the novices would be dismissed. It seems to me that in terms of their sexuality, Jesuit novices fell into one of two categories. Either we were integrating our sexuality into a maturing and wholesome personality, or we were suppressing it, sometimes at enormous personal cost. If the second, the problem could well emerge later with sometimes tragic consequences, such as the abuse uncovered in a Jesuit boarding school for native children in northern Ontario.

The third vow, obedience, was the cornerstone of the entire Jesuit program, practised in the minutiae of the many novitiate customs, bells, appointments, orders, spying, secrecy and all the rest. St. Ignatius had been a soldier. He expected his followers to be obedient even to the letter of the law. There were horror stories, likely apocryphal, of novices being ordered to plant vegetable gardens upside down. A Jesuit superior stood in the place of Christ. If the superior gave an order, it was to be obeyed by the subject "like a corpse," which I took to mean there was not even to be a twitch of hesitation or reluctance.

The Jesuit structure within which such obedience is demanded is an impressive one. The Jesuits world-wide are divided into 120 jurisdictions or provinces, now totalling about 23,000 members, down from 36,000 in 1965. The structure starts with the local superior, usually called the rector, ascends to the provincial, then to the Superior General in Rome and then to the Pope. All in all, the Jesuit order was and, despite the drop in numbers, still is a substantial religious machine. But sometimes we ordinary Jesuits felt like small cogs in the wheel. The emotional risk in the vow of obedience was that we put our life into somebody else's hands. At a moment's notice we could be commanded when to go, where to go and how to get there. In actuality, Jesuit obedience does not operate all that militaristically and in my own experience, especially after the fifteen-year period of training was over, was exercised with charity and intelligence.

The three perpetual vows were the culmination of the novitiate training but they were not the height of Ignatian spirituality. That was represented by the three degrees of humility and more especially the third degree, which was not an intense interrogation but a spiritual ideal - the summit of St. Ignatius's Exercises. I have no doubt the third degree is a rare and subtle ascetic ideal. I also have no doubt that I never understood it. And I don't think I was alone. I never understood it because, in my opinion, it was never explained properly.

In rough and ready terms, the third degree comes down to this: when faced with two courses of action, all other things being equal, one chooses the more difficult course because that resembles Christ's choice of the cross. How does this work in practice? Not well. Consider a practical example. I want to take a shower. There are two showers from which to choose. One works well and the other one doesn't. Should I choose the defective shower because in so choosing I practise the third degree? Another example: the main course at dinner is liver and bacon. I like bacon and hate liver, always have, always will. Should I choose the liver? This last example did not work well for me in practice. By the time the liver and bacon would reach me at table in the novitiate, usually all the bacon was gone and so was the chance to practise the third degree.

There were other discussions about the third degree that verged on the bizarre. The famous Jesuit prayer *Suscipe*, sung at Jesuit vow ceremonies, contains the line "Take my memory, my understanding, and my entire will." So the question would arise, under certain circumstances would it be appropriate to ask God to take our minds and render us insane? Just to ask the question is to realize how unhealthy spirituality could become in inexperienced hands in the intense climate of the novitiate.

Finally the last day of the novitiate, September 8, 1945, dawned for two of my fellow novices and me. It was our vow day. I had several conversations with the master of novices concerning my continuing doubts and misgivings about whether I should proceed to pronounce perpetual vows. The master did not try to convince me to stay. Nor did he say anything that suggested I was not a suitable candidate for vows. So the decision came down to me alone, and I decided to go ahead.

More than fifty years later, it is easier to disentangle the elements of that decision than it would have been to articulate them then. I was not certain that God was calling me to be a Jesuit but after the two years of novitiate, the probabilities came down on the side that He was. Even more compelling were the images that came up so frequently during the novitiate training, such as the story from Luke (9:57-62) about would-be followers of Jesus - the rich young man who turned away from Christ at the last minute (and perhaps lost his soul) and the other young man who put his hand to the plough and decided to turn back. Could I risk rejecting Christ and risking damnation? Could I let down my mother, my fellow-Jesuits and all those people who were expecting me to proceed? And if I did turn back, what would I do? I don't say all those motives were clear at the time. But they were all operating at some level and they carried enough emotional weight to impel me forward.

And so at mass, with the early morning sunlight streaming through the chapel's rose-coloured windows, the whole Jesuit community was assembled before the altar banked with red and white flowers, bright in the light of blazing candles. With the music soaring and the choir singing "O Lord take and receive my memory, my understanding, and my entire will," I mounted the altar steps, knelt before the rector, bowed my head and in my new Jesuit cassock, recited the vow formula, "... *ego voveo paupertatem, castitatem et oboedientiam perpetuam in Societate Jesu....*" It was a day of rejoicing. Mother was there, though not Stafford, and after the service, all our families and those of us who took vows breakfasted together in the refectory - where we were allowed to talk at the meal for the first time in two years. There was an enormous feast at noon, Jesuits being famous for meals on special feast days, where the number of desserts reflects the rank of the feast. After the meal there were sports and entertainment. I had been on probation for two years. Now the Jesuits had accepted me as a member of their famous company, which meant I could wear a biretta on my head, put S.J. after my name and was entitled to be called Mister.

Sometime in the evening, I went alone into the chapel which was lit only by the ruby glow of the sanctuary lamp. I knelt before the Blessed Sacrament and tried to pray. Why, after so glorious a day, did I feel slightly uneasy and unsure? Why did the day now ending feel like so many Christmas days in my past - disappointing? Why was the split still there between the way I felt about myself and the way I wanted others to feel about me? Taking perpetual vows in the Society of Jesus had not healed the split. In some way I could not then foresee, vows had only made it worse.

6

CRUELTY AND PARANOIA

After the excitement of vow day, the next stage of Jesuit formation was only a few steps beyond the end of the novitiate walk - in an institutional red brick building called the juniorate. In some ways it was a different world. Instead of looking inward all the time, we now looked outward at the exciting world of books, especially the world of the classics. Greek, Latin and English were the staples of the juniorate curriculum, with some history and mathematics thrown in for variety. One junior described the course as a marvellous nineteenth-century English university education, the type that Arnold Toynbee believed his was among the last generation to receive.

Instead of toiling away in an open ascetory, we now worked in curtained cubicles. We read Aristotle's treatise on rhetoric, wherein he describes how to arrange arguments for maximum effect and how to disguise weak arguments as strong. Many modern politicians could read Aristotle with profit. We read Vergil, Horace, Sophocles, Euripides and Cicero - my favourite - all in the original. How challenging it was to translate into the language of a modern-day criminal lawyer a courtroom presentation of Cicero, perhaps his address to the jury as he defended the murderer Milo.

I learned to appreciate the clarity and precision of the Latin language and I believe that the study of classical Latin is an enormous help in constructing a good English sentence. Of course we studied Shakespeare and other great English writers such as Milton, Keats, Shelley, Wordsworth, and Edmund Burke, not to mention Cardinal Newman who wrote *Second Spring*. Laurence Braceland taught us English composition and, to my astonishment, gave us our heads. We wrote poetry, short stories, film-scripts - the works. "Make me sing in the bathtub," Braceland would exhort us and with enthusiasm we did our best.

I wish I could remember only the positive and enthusiastic aspects of our two years in the juniorate, challenged by the great writers of history. Unfortunately there is a shadow side to the story. The shadow was Father Leo Nelligan, dean of the juniorate. I don't know what personal emotional baggage he brought into the Society of Jesus, but by the time he was appointed dean, Nelligan (then in his sixties) was a religious martinet, pure and simple. His own religious observance was as regular and rigid as that of a Marine commandant. And that is how he ran the juniorate, like a boot camp.

So far as most juniors were concerned, Nelligan was remote, taciturn, ensconced in his room smoking his pipe and incessantly pounding his typewriter. He taught the plays of Shakespeare and some of the longer poems of Milton such as *Lycidas*, in a competent bloodless manner. He emphasized picayune analysis rather than emotion and imagination. Under Nelligan we picked away at the soliloquies of Shakespeare the way a pigeon picks at dry bread. He sometimes snubbed those juniors who did not measure up to his standards or whom he did not like. On more than one occasion I experienced Nelligan's obduracy first hand. Once when I had tried to memorize a long chunk of Greek poetry in the original, I went to Nelligan's room to make my presentation. He lit his pipe, remained at his typewriter and brusquely told me to begin. After reciting about fifty lines, with Nelligan continuing to type, I faltered, tried to start again, then stuttered to a stop. Without looking up, Nelligan told me to come back when I was prepared.

A man of Nelligan's temperament could be devastating during reading at table. Except for feast days when conversation is permitted, a book is read aloud from a pulpit during meals in a Jesuit refectory. After more than half a century, I still remember the book being read when I entered the novitiate, a biography of Philip II of Spain. Nelligan was the *repetatur*. If the reader made a mistake in pronunciation or interpretation, Nelligan would order him to stop and repeat, his orders often sounding like a fusillade from a shotgun - a nerve-wracking experience, especially for uncertain or weak readers.

Finally a rumour spread among the juniors that the beadle, the juniorate equivalent of the admonitor in the novitiate, had complained to the Jesuit provincial's assistant about Nelligan's bullying. Whether the rumour was accurate or not (I think it was), nothing was done. Father Leo Nelligan was left in office to carry on his destructive formation of impressionable young men who were taught that Nelligan's voice was the voice of Christ. In the many years that I remained a Jesuit I never encountered a more unkind "brother in Christ" than Leo Nelligan. Under his regime my chronic insomnia, bad enough in the novitiate, became worse. In desperation, unable to face Nelligan and a full day's study after a sleepless night, I wrangled a few sleeping pills from the Brother Infirmarian. They were Seconals and they were the first of thousands of sleeping pills I would consume in the coming years.

Then in June 1948, we closed our books, packed our trunks and prepared for the next phase in our Jesuit training, the study of philosophy. First, we made an eight-day retreat in silence, an annual obligation for all Jesuits, and spent a few weeks relaxing at the Jesuit villa on Lake Joseph in the Muskokas. Then to Toronto and the Jesuit Seminary, often referred to as "403" because the address was 403 Wellington Street. This housed both the philosophers and the theologians, the latter group approaching ordination to the priesthood.

The old Jesuit Seminary was a mammoth red brick turreted building near the Toronto railroad tracks and the waterfront where *The Globe and Mail* is now located. It was an historic building, constructed for the Attorney-General of Upper Canada in 1837, and in it the Prince of Wales, later Edward VII, attended a ball in 1860. It eventually fell into the hands of the Sisters of Loretto. When the Depression deepened in the thirties, the good sisters found the building, with its draughty rabbit-warrens and dark cul-de-sacs, too expensive to maintain, and tried without success to find a buyer. Finally, so the story goes, they prayed to the Jesuit Martyrs to find a buyer foolish enough to take the place off their hands. Their prayers were answered. The Jesuits bought it. And so for the next quarter-century, Jesuit scholastics, both philosophers and theologians, tried to cope with the grime, the grit and the grunting from shunting trains at the nearby railroad tracks.

I began philosophy with high hopes. Unfortunately, my hopes were dashed by the program itself, and then by a personal problem I had not foreseen. First, the program. As if the content was not abstract enough, all the classes were in Latin. Most of the professors spoke a serviceable Latin. So did some of the student philosophers. But many of us neither understood the language adequately nor spoke it well. In addition, there was a difficulty in the whole approach to the subject. At the Jesuit seminary (and I expect the same applied to most Catholic seminaries in the world) we did not read philosophy the way we read Shakespeare - with an open mind. We were not so much *reading* philosophy as *doing* philosophy, and the philosophy we were doing was Aristotilian-Thomistic. Our teacher was St. Thomas Aquinas, our textbook his monumental *Summa Theologica*. All the elaborate structure of the classroom lectures, the carefully constructed chain of objections and the syllogisms resembled nothing so much as a phony wrestling match. The arena was set, the fix was in, the outcome known in advance.

Yet like those well-rehearsed wrestlers, we went through all the motions four days a week for three years. We rigorously followed the thesis method - a statement to be proved, a summary of the problem and a line-up of adversaries and objections. The adversaries were always the same suspects, Descartes, Hume, Kant, Spinoza, Hegel and Locke. But this was strictly a straw-man operation. Most Jesuit scholastics never read these authors and I doubt that many of the professors had read them extensively. We just lined up these "pagan" philosophers like decoys, then constructed our own syllogisms and proofs based on St. Thomas and shot all our adversaries dead every time.

So for three years we plodded through dozens of theses in metaphysics, epistemology, cosmology and the history of philosophy, with the outcome always rigged in advance. I don't claim there was no value in this exercise. There is something both logical and orderly about the thesis method. Many years later as host of an open-line radio program in Montreal, I would use the summary of the problem under discussion, called the *status quaestionis,* to frame short clear questions for my listeners. Anyone who gets the structure of the thesis method into his bloodstream will think more clearly, but it doesn't necessarily make him a philosopher.

Still, what happened outside the classroom at 403 was for me more upsetting than what didn't happen inside it. When I first arrived at the philosophate, I ran into a wall of hostility that I could neither comprehend nor overcome. I am perfectly willing to admit that by this time I had developed a kind of chronic paranoia.

If I walked into a roomful of people, I just naturally assumed that most of them would not like me. But this attitude could not account for the coldness I experienced in Toronto from many of my fellow scholastics, both philosophers and theologians, from some of my professors and from the rector himself. I felt bewildered and alone. My insomnia became almost unbearable and I could only get so many pills.

It was only years later that a friend told me what may have caused this antagonism. Before arriving in Toronto, while still on holiday in Muskoka, I had had a long conversation with another scholastic from my own year. We agreed that we would try to obey the rules in Toronto as meticulously as we had obeyed them at Guelph, that we did not want to lose our "first fervour" and that we would heed the master's warning about becoming more slack as the formation became more free. It is difficult now to reconstruct a conversation that occurred more than fifty years ago, but I may well have expressed concern about slackness at the Jesuit Seminary in Toronto.

In any event, the conversation was overheard by other scholastics and apparently they construed my remarks to mean that I was coming to Toronto to lead a reformation on rules and regulations (shades of my ill-fated term as admonitor). Apparently, too, this information passed through the grapevine to the whole Jesuit community including the rector. No wonder they acted with some wariness, not to say outright hostility. And I reacted the only way I knew how, with my own resentment and aggression. This was still another painful example of the split between the way I felt inside and the way I wanted others to perceive me.

Meanwhile as I was muddling along by myself in the dark, another friend, a philosopher in my own year, threw me a lifeline. Edgar Burns from Montreal was the most popular Jesuit in our group. He had a stocky athletic build, a mop of reddish hair and a flair for public speaking. He also had a remarkable quality - he truly liked others and somehow made them feel better about themselves. He lived a simple and natural spirituality. Edgar was not much interested in the letter of the law but he had an unerring instinct for recognizing its spirit.

Of Edgar Burns' many friends and admirers, I was only an admirer, until one evening after community litanies in the chapel, he whispered to me to come up to his room. I was astonished, partly because the period following litanies until after breakfast was called "sacred silence" when no one speaks except for an emergency. Also, I was not accustomed to invitations of that sort. But, in this friendless place, Edgar was holding out the hand of friendship and I grabbed it.

Sitting in Edgar's room, I began to experience a feeling of relief and gratitude. Here was someone who apparently cared for me. It was like a glass of refreshing water after a long thirst. Then came another surprise - Edgar offered me a cigarette. Smoking was forbidden without special permission, which was rarely given. But I took the cigarette with a conspiratorial feeling that I had made it, if only temporarily, to another level, a more humane level. I had a friend who wanted to share with me.

Many a night I went to Edgar's room and we talked through sacred silence until after midnight. On Thursdays we often took the ferry to the Island, my favourite place in Toronto, where we stretched out on the fresh green grass and gazed at Lake Ontario shimmering in the sunshine. We read the Toronto newspapers and smoked Philip Morris cigarettes - both against the rules. Edgar Burns saved my sanity that final year in philosophy. His friendship was a grace for which I shall always be grateful. Since 1951, Edgar has been attached to the Canadian Jesuit mission in Darjeeling where he has committed his life to the poor of India. He is an outstanding Jesuit and I am glad he was my friend.

At the end of the three-year philosophy course (I managed to pass my oral examination in Latin) my classmates and I speculated about where we were going next. Most of us were going to teach for a period of three years at one of the ten high schools and colleges the English Canadian Jesuits staffed from Halifax to Regina. This three-year period was called Regency. On the morning of July 31, the feast of St. Ignatius, the appointments, called the *Status*, were pinned up on the bulletin board. Feverishly we all looked for our names. When I found mine, I learned that, ironically, I was going back to the place I had spent the loneliest year of my life, Regiopolis College, in good old grey Kingston.

7

FAILURE AND SUCCESS

When I arrived in Kingston in August, I knew I was to teach English in the middle grades and history in the dreaded Grade Thirteen, the equivalent of first year college. I had had no training in teaching and little in history, although I had taken a couple of undergraduate history courses at the University of Toronto during my philosophy years.

In the first week of September, the students, including sixty who would be boarders, descended upon us. Not a few came from wealthy homes in South America and Toronto. We had the impression that these rich parents wanted the Jesuits, famous for discipline, to take their children off their hands and make men of them. I came to know these older boarders well because I was put in charge of the senior dormitory. This dormitory with its military beds and red coverlets was where I had begun my own sojourn as a Regi student just eight years earlier.

Being in charge meant a full day. I rose at 5:30, showered and dressed, went down to chapel for a few short prayers, meditated for an hour, rang a bell and rousted up my thirty-odd charges. I herded them to mass at 7:30, then had a quick breakfast with the Jesuit community. My old recruiting friend, Father Joe Driscoll, was now my assistant superior. I taught a history class at 8:30, followed by a class in English, took a break for lunch and taught two more English classes in the afternoon. Recreation at 3:30 was sometimes spent with the students or watching football practice. Regi was a good sports school and I enjoyed the games hard-fought with other regional teams.

Sometimes I presided over study hall at 5:00. Supper was at 6:00, where I took my turn reading at table. In the evening, a short recreation was followed by class preparation, litanies in the chapel at 9:00, then back up to the dormitory. It was time to herd my charges into bed without bedlam or too much noise, or the rector, Father Clem Crusoe, would make inquiries. Dorm lights were out at 9:45, after which I hoped a water fight or some other chicanery would not break out. Then I retired to my room to hit the books for next day's class and was in bed by 11:30 for six hours' sleep before it all started again at 5:30. Unfortunately I seldom slept for six hours, even with the occasional sleeping pill. Insomnia still weighed me down like a leaden backpack so that several times during my three years at Regi, I ended up in Hotel Dieu Hospital with the flu and a high temperature, the result of my system signalling stress and fatigue.

Over New Year's, 1952, the rector generously allowed me to go home to Hastings to visit my mother. I knew she was worried about the hardware business and Staff's drinking. She had tried to keep her concern out of her cheery weekly letters, but just recently she had written: "The more I think about selling the business the better it would surely be for Staff. He certainly requires more guidance and experience with an older man. He is in a rut over here. I can't see any smart business men in the town, not one that you could say has the shrewdness and ability Daddy had." On the afternoon of New Year's Eve, on my twenty-seventh birthday, I arrived home to find Mother looking strained and older. She was being treated for a heart problem which, typically, she never discussed with me because she did not want to upset me. But we did talk about the financial situation at the store and Stafford's drinking. I reassured her as best I could, then walked across the Trent River bridge to the hardware store to see Stafford. He had obviously been drinking, and I reacted much as I had to Dad - with anger, resentment and fear. I expressed my concern but my brother responded, as I should have known he would, with sullen silence.

That night at supper there was a little birthday party for me. Stafford was there with his wife, Sue, a gentle reserved young woman, and their two little children, John and Michael. Sue was very attached to her mother-in-law. At dessert time Mother brought in the candle-topped birthday cake, my favourite - rich, dark chocolate. I kept up a good front but felt anxious because I did not know how to cope with Mother's failing health, Stafford's drinking or the unpaid suppliers' bills at the store. Just before she went to bed, I reassured Mother that after mass in the morning we would all have a chat and, one way or another, come up with a plan to work things out.

I slept fitfully. In the morning I heard Stafford get up and go to Mother's room. Suddenly he cried out and I instantly felt I knew why. I rose, threw on a bathrobe and hurried into Mother's bedroom, the one she had always shared with Dad. She was lying on the bed, looking worn but serene, her rosary in her hand. She had died quietly during the night.

I immediately called Father Garvey, still the parish priest. He could not have been more supportive, kind and generous, then and later. I then called the undertaker and some friends and relatives. Then I went to mass, as Mother had planned. The shocked congregation prayed for the repose of her soul as I knelt in the sanctuary where I had spent so much time as an altar boy. I was in a dazed feeling of apprehension tinctured with guilt. Had I been the support for my mother I should have been or had I let her down? And that is how I went through the next few days, anxious, uneasy, with a sense of failure.

Still, I took charge of the funeral arrangements, as Stafford's own daze was fuelled by alcohol. I was criticized by one or two of Mother's friends for buying an inexpensive coffin. But it seemed to me that Stafford and his family could make better use of the money we would have spent for an expensive coffin.

After her funeral, attended by so many in the community where she had lived all her married life, my mother was buried beside my father. I said good-bye to them in the Catholic cemetery at the top of the steep hill overlooking the Norwood Road and the frozen Trent River beyond the shuttered summer cottages. It was a cold and wintry day as we stood beside her open grave. Together she and Dad had done their best. Mother was a kind and gentle woman of deep faith. She had loved me and was proud of me. In my own way, I had done my best to return her love. Sometimes I still wonder about our life as a family. But what really matters now are not the questions but the love.

After Mother's funeral I returned to Kingston with a heavy spirit. She was dead - perhaps of worry that I should have dealt with. Stafford was drinking heavily and I didn't know how to deal with it, and Dad's hardware store was heading for collapse. It was in this desolate frame of mind that I plodded through the next few months. I was especially concerned about my Grade Thirteen history tests, a set of examinations drawn up and marked by the educational authorities and constituting the standard for schools such as Regiopolis in Ontario.

As it turned out, I had plenty of reason to be concerned. After a vacation at the Jesuit villa on Lac de l'Achigan in the Laurentians, and our annual eight-day retreat at Loyola College in Montreal, I returned to Regi in early August just in time for the publication of the Grade

Thirteen results in *The Whig-Standard*. My history results were a disaster. Two of my students had failed. The marks of the rest were mediocre. I was summoned to the rector's office and informed that if I could not do better, I would be removed from my history class and perhaps from the school altogether.

I was shattered, but instead of throwing in the towel, I decided, as I had many years before in Hastings, that by God I would show them! So I looked for and found all the Grade Thirteen history exams from previous years, structured these around the assigned text book, *Colony to Nation* by Professor Lower of Queen's University, enriched this mix with my own reading, and walked into my first class in September with a course designed to knock examinations for a loop. Ruthlessly, I weeded out a couple of students I didn't think would make it. When three or four students were late for class, I brought them back on the weekend and ordered them to write a two-hour paper, while I sat with my feet propped on a desk, drinking Coke and smoking cigarettes (shades of Father Leo Nelligan). These draconian measures paid off handsomely. All my nineteen students made honours, fourteen received first-class honours and one achieved a mark of 95. These results, Professor Donald Creighton, later Sir John A.'s biographer, told me were probably the best in the province. In any event, they saved my teaching career at Regi.

Life with the Jesuit community also became more relaxed, although our superiors seemed to see themselves as mentors rather than friends. Their primary responsibility was to form us in the image of St. Ignatius as they saw him. But I did make some good friends in the community. One was John Moore, whom I often visited after lights-out in the dormitory. He had a wry sense of humour, and laced his scotch nightcaps with milk in deference to his ulcer. I also made friends outside the community. Two in particular, the O'Connors, made a difference in my life then and even more so later on.

Maurice O'Connor was a psychiatrist with his own practice. He was also on the staff at Kingston Penitentiary and Queen's University. His wife, Jean, a warm and generous woman filled with quiet laughter and common sense, was the head of the Women's Auxiliary at Regi. They had three children, Maureen, Brenda and Fergus. The O'Connors were a prominent Catholic family in Kingston. Maurice's father was a doctor and his brother Fergus was a pediatrician. They had a great many relatives and not surprisingly a great many friends.

To my amazement and gratitude, I gradually found myself being taken into the O'Connor family circle. One entrée was their son, Fergus, who was in my English class and whose interest in writing I encouraged. He would later become a successful high school English teacher. Tentatively I began to allow myself to think that maybe Jean and Maurice actually liked me. I was invited frequently, often with other Jesuits, to their summer home on Loughborough Lake. I relished these visits the way a sugar freak relishes maple syrup. I had never before experienced such an easy, relaxed, loving family circle. It was a new experience and a rich one.

As for the many boys I taught and supervised over my three years at Regi, my respect for them was reciprocated, and some may even have liked me - especially those in the debating society which I moderated. There was great camaraderie in the society and they won many debates. Of course, teaching Grade Thirteen history in a way that was exciting and provoked enthusiasm was a challenging and rewarding experience. I often met the challenge by building the narrative around strong historical personalities. And to read English writing assignments that sparkled with imagination and verve often made me "sing in the bathtub." A couple of my students would go on to Harvard and do well in medicine. Patrick Lesage, an unassuming English student, would become Chief Justice of the Ontario Supreme Court, Trial Division, and preside over the notorious Bernardo murder trial.

Busy as I was, I tried to keep up my interest in current events, driving with other Jesuit scholastics to the Jesuit University at Syracuse to visit and watch the Senator Joe McCarthy hearings on television. Sometimes after the dormitory lights were out, I would turn on the radio low to listen to the great soaring, chiselled speeches of the Democratic presidential candidate, Adlai Stevenson, one of my political heroes.

Also during my time at Regi, Stafford moved to Kingston with his family. His wife, Sue, had found Mother's death so upsetting that it was affecting her health. With all these difficulties, Stafford was doing his best to hold things together. Just before the move, Father Garvey, still the village priest and a great support to all of us during this trying period, had written: "Your good brother has not touched a drink in nearly a month and has been at Mass and Holy Communion every day since the first of the month. Please God he will persevere in his good work and resolutions." Stafford had sold the hardware store and I helped him get a position with Vandervoort's, an established hardware concern on Princess Street. He would be a valued employee with them for thirty years. During those years he had a good marriage and raised three boys, all of whom have done well. Occasionally, just briefly, Staff and I seemed to connect. To my astonishment, one night after supper at his home, be began to cry. He said he blamed himself for our mother's death. I tried to reassure him as best I could, but I don't think it helped much.

8

PRIESTHOOD AND SEX

In the early summer of 1945, I said good-bye to Regiopolis for the second and last time and headed back to 403, the Jesuit Seminary in Toronto. I was to begin a four-year course in theology which would culminate in ordination to the priesthood at the end of the third year. But first we had a holiday in the Muskokas at the Jesuit villa, an ancient yellow frame hotel bought in the Depression. It was high on a bluff overlooking the blue waters of Lake Joseph. There we enjoyed a relaxed life of boating, swimming, rugged volleyball, savoury meals, beer and music in the evening, lots of cards (mostly bridge), long walks in the woods to Clear Lake, and conversation, forming new friendships or deepening old ones. Sometimes early in the morning before the mist rose from the water, I would head out in a Peterborough skiff with two companions, Bill Ryan and Ed McGuire, and row all day to Bracebridge and back, returning so sore and sunburned I could scarcely get undressed. Then a few days later we would do it all over again. What was I trying to prove? Whatever it was, those Muskoka trips were a rough metaphor for my own journey. Without quite knowing why, I just kept rowing for dear life.

From the fluffy clouds and blue waters of the Muskokas to the grime and grit of the old Jesuit Seminary was only a few hours' car ride, but it was a different world. In the sprawling complex of 403, we were assigned rooms in cul-de-sacs in sections with names like Glass Alley, Eskimo Flat or the Band Box. The external format of the theology course resembled that in philosophy, proving innumerable propositions through the thesis method, again all in Latin.

It would be difficult to describe the sheer volume of material presented in lecture after lecture, week after week, month after month, during our four-year theology course which was based upon the monumental works of St. Thomas Aquinas. Besides our textbooks, there was a blizzard of hand-outs in the major disciplines such as

Dogmatic Theology (the study of the nature of God), Moral Theology (the examination of the moral quality of human acts), Canon Law (the study of the rules and regulations established by the church governing everything from whether a cleric should wear a beard to how he should treat his housekeeper).

For weeks in Moral Theology we discussed stealing and restitution. How much did you have to steal before it became a mortal sin? If you stole something, did you have to give it back if returning it incriminated you? Was cheating on your taxes stealing? What were the circumstances in which you could keep what you stole? These would all be relevant questions for a priest who one day would have a congregation of bank robbers. We dissected restitution the way a pathologist dissects a cadaver but never in my ten years of hearing confessions did the matter come up. My argument here is not with the study of restitution itself but the ludicrous emphasis placed upon it.

In some of the other theology courses such as Canon Law, this emphasis on impractical matters was even more absurd. Could a cleric wear a beard and how full a beard could it be? Did wearing a contraceptive have any bearing on the mortal sin of intercourse outside marriage? We weighed the gravity of venial and mortal sins the way a pharmacist weighs drugs in a prescription. For instance, the sanctuary lamp in front of the altar should be lit at all times. If it were carelessly allowed to go out, would that be a venial sin? How long would it have to stay out before the venial sin became a mortal sin?

In order to hear confessions, a priest must obtain jurisdiction from the territorial diocese in which he is located. But what if the priest were in an aircraft and didn't know where he was in relationship to the diocese below him? If that priest heard someone's confession in the air, would the confession be invalid? And then came the famous treatise on *De Sextu*, all the sexual sins in the book, including bestiality. When it came to sexual sins, there were no small matters. If you stole ten dollars, that might well be a small matter and therefore a venial sin. But when it came to sex.... Say you had been married for years; if you touched yourself alone and deliberately took pleasure in it, that, brother, was a mortal sin. We analyzed hundreds of sins the way a scientist analyzes atomic particles. Yet I doubt whether a priest in the active ministry would ever use more than ten percent of what he had learned so meticulously and laboriously in Moral Theology. Certainly I didn't. As for the infamous treatise on *De Sextu*, ninety-nine percent of effectively hearing confessions on sexual matters came not from theology but from common sense.

There was one shining exception to the otherwise plodding treatises in theology. Studying scripture was like arriving in an oasis after a parched trek through the desert. Father David Stanley in New Testament, Father Roderick MacKenzie in Old Testament, both renowned scholars in the biblical world, were, far and away, the best Jesuit teachers I ever had. For me, the Bible, to the extent I was familiar with it at all, was largely a dead, not to say threatening book. Fathers MacKenzie and Stanley brought the Bible alive and made it as relevant and as compelling as the morning's headlines.

Instead of long stretches of impenetrable prose studded with contradictions, impossibilities and unknown allusions, our guides took us back to the Bible as an oral tradition transmitted by raconteurs around the rising smoke of glowing campfires. This was a far cry from the literalists and fundamentalists who years later would call my open-line radio program and explain to me that God dictated every inspired word of the Bible to scribes (who presumably were experts in shorthand if not in word processors). These campfire narratives took many forms - poetry, epics, short stories, speeches, long narratives, allegories, and it was impossible to understand the Bible unless one understood the literary forms the writer was using, forms appropriate for the listeners of his day. Of course the Bible is filled with myths. That is not the problem. The problem is that so many modern readers of the Bible understand myth to be fiction. Indeed the narrative may be a fiction. But the underlying truth clothed by the narrative is not. The narrative that God created the world over a period of seven days may not be "true" in any literal sense of our understanding of time. But the truth is that a force outside the world, "God," in fact created the world. That is what the writer was trying to convey, whatever the literary form he used to convey it.

Almost as exciting as scripture was the history course I was following at the University of Toronto with my friend Jacques Monet, later to become one of Canada's most distinguished historians. When my superiors had first offered me the opportunity to begin a university degree, I chose English as my major. A senior Jesuit, Father McInerney, who was an expert in Shakespeare, asked me, "Why English?" I told him I wanted to become a writer. "If that is so," he said, "the *last* thing you want to take is English. Unless they're interested in fiction or poetry, most would-be writers have nothing to write about. They have nothing to say. If you want to write, follow a course that will give you something to write about." I thought about it, took his advice and began courses for a degree program in Canadian history. I have never regretted my choice and have always been grateful for Father McInerney's wise advice. In fact, my first book, published in 1967, was a biography of Ontario premier Mitch Hepburn.

By the beginning of my third year in theology, September 1956, it was time to think about the most serious step I would ever take, ordination to the priesthood, scheduled for the following June. My old doubts and anxieties about whether to proceed emerged again more acutely. Fortunately, there was a new spiritual director for the scholastics, Father Gordon George, S.J. Gordie George, a native of the Ottawa Valley, was a stocky Jesuit with a ready grin and a consuming interest in politics, psychology, and what makes a person tick. Friendly, accessible, supportive, yet deeply spiritual, he was as knowledgeable about Eisenhower's republicanism as he was about the writings of the psychoanalyst Karen Horney. Previously, Father George had been a member of the editorial staff of *America,* a prestigious public affairs review published by the Jesuits in New York City. In fact, he encouraged me to write an article for *America,* which I did, and so had my first piece, a profile of the Canadian prime minister, Louis St. Laurent, published in the United States.

As ordination approached, its solemnity and gravity became lost in the frenzy of preparations, including making guest lists, designing and printing invitations, learning how to say low and high mass with every flutter of the hands and bow of the head measured in millimeters, and rushing out to have photographs taken at Toronto's premier photography studio, Ashley and Crippen. Then in the evening, after the day's rushing around, I would have long talks with Father George in his room about my doubts and hesitations. The irony was obvious when these doubts were viewed next to the very preparations in which I was so frantically engaged.

A compassionate and insightful man, Father George took much the same position about my ordination to the priesthood as my master of novices had taken about my perpetual vows. He did not urge me to stay, but he saw no impediment to my going forward, and he later wrote about this period to my then Jesuit superior in Cleveland: "Father McKenty responded so well to the counselling I was able to give him that neither he nor I had the slightest doubts about his suitability for ordination." But I still wonder why some Jesuit friend or perceptive spiritual director such as Gordie George, aware of a pattern of doubt and uncertainty that had plagued my vocation for so many years, did not just advise me to pack it in and try something else. The answer is not as obvious as it may seem. For one thing, I had satisfactorily completed thirteen years of rigorous Jesuit training. At some level of my consciousness, I still believed that God was calling me to become a Jesuit priest. However, there is no question that in this proposition lay a basic defect of the decision process - the "call" had originated elsewhere and I was never able to internalize it and make it solidly my own. Instead I relied on the Jesuit structure which had flourished for more than four centuries and which substituted for my inability to establish an inner sense of direction.

Then there were images operating at another level of consciousness, of the young man who lifted his hand from the plough with the job half done and the other young man who turned away because he had other priorities. What had happened to them? Were they failures? Were they burning in hell while the bird picked the sand from the beach? Finally, at still another level of consciousness, if I did not become a Jesuit priest, what would I do? Could I survive out there? What would my relatives and friends think? Was there a positive divine sign in this dynamic leading me forward? In fact, in a curious way, the strongest forces moving me forward were probably negative. Considering all the circumstances and our talks together, it was not incumbent upon Father George to tell me to pack up and take off. The decision was mine and I decided to proceed.

We were to be ordained in the chapel of the Jesuit seminary on the first Sunday of June 1957 by his Grace James Charles McGuigan, Archbishop of Toronto. It was a warm, sunny day. The chapel was filled with guests and friends, including Stafford and his family, and to my surprise, Father Garvey, our old parish priest who had supported Stafford and me so generously through all our ups and downs. The ordination ceremony where the ordinands spend part of the time lying face down in the sanctuary is a moving and impressive one. At the end, as Archbishop McGuigan blessed the congregation on his way out, he turned to the newly-ordained priests and murmured with a smile, "Pray every day to be faithful." After a major step of this kind in my life I always waited for an inner sign that I had done the right thing. It never came.

More exciting than the ordination itself was my first high mass, to be said in my old parish in Hastings the following Sunday. I had asked my former novice master, Father Cloran, to speak at my mass. Whatever his shortcomings as master, and I am certain he did not seek the position, he was a straight-shooter, a spiritual man, and had always treated me with kindness and fairness. As mass time approached, trying to sort out my feelings, I walked up and down in front of the church where I had served as altar boy. On the one hand, I felt a kind of nervous elation that I had become a Jesuit priest, no little accomplishment, and was now back where it had all started, sharing my triumph with so many friends. On the other hand, there was a niggling suspicion that all this frenetic celebration was happening at a superficial level. There was something unreal about the young Jesuit in the black cassock whom so many were congratulating. Only he knew that just underneath the outer success crouched the anxiety and fear - the snarling dogs, barely held at bay.

Then it was time to robe for mass. During the service, with Father Garvey and Father Cloran beside me, I gave my brother and his family my first priestly blessing, thanked everyone, and said a few words about what I owed my parents for this day. Then we all walked over past the cenotaph to the town hall for a splendid banquet. The warm, friendly spirit of the occasion reminded me of those suppers in church basements so long ago when my parents took us to sit down with Protestants and we all feasted together.

After my first high mass and a few weeks in Muskoka, I returned to 403 to begin my fourth and final year in theology. No sooner had I returned to the theologate than the snarling dogs leapt into consciousness. I dreaded their presence and I was stunned by their message: I had made a dreadful mistake; I should never have become a priest; I had now made an irreversible commitment that would lock me in for the rest of my life; I was in prison and there was no way out. I was in a panic which Father George, who had been made rector, recognized as soon as I went to his room to see him. I was so agitated that he made me lie down on his bed. Gradually I regained some calm and we agreed we would talk on a regular basis.

More holiday time in the Muskokas restored some of my tranquillity. It was our first summer as active priests and most Sundays we went out to neighbouring parishes. Sometimes we went to summer missions, little white clapboard chapels clinging to the steep hillsides overlooking the sparkling waters of the Muskoka lakes. We gave our first sermons and had our first experience of hearing confessions. Initially there was a kind of curiosity, even voyeurism, involved in hearing confessions. But it didn't last long. Listening to confessions, one after the other, usually interminable litanies of bad thoughts, uncharitable desires, distractions in prayer, missing mass on Sunday, became about as interesting as listening to a clock ticking.

In theology class we had been told that the Holy Spirit would help us forget any material we heard in the confessional. I can't imagine why we needed the help of the Holy Spirit. The material was eminently forgettable with, in my own experience, one notable exception. One Sunday morning a young woman, somewhat nervous and hesitant, came into my confessional. She explained that she had just recently been married, and then went on to describe, in a barely audible voice, that on at least one occasion, her pleasure during lovemaking with her husband had been so intense that she had momentarily lost consciousness. Was this a serious sin? I assured her it was not a sin of any kind and I could sense her relief. Had I been more experienced as confessor I should have told her to thank God. In any event, despite His/Her best efforts over the years, the Holy Spirit has never obliterated that particular confession from my memory.

After theology classes began again in the fall, Father George, who by this time had been appointed Jesuit Provincial, and who continued to support me without stint, arranged for me to see a psychiatrist on a regular basis to try to deal with my anxiety and insomnia. At the end of my last and uneventful year in theology I was invited to go to Kitchener to speak at the first mass of one of my close friends, Vic Traynor. When it came to preaching, I had a lot going for me - an expressive voice, good presence and well-worked material. Why, then, did I many times feel perplexed and uncomfortable after giving my sermons, even when listeners were congratulating me on them? I think because the words the congregation heard, theologically sound I am sure, did not jibe with my feelings about those words in my heart. The ball did not go smack into the glove. There was a feeling of dis-ease that left me vaguely uncomfortable.

Not to worry. I delivered my sermon at Vic's first mass in Kitchener and spent the afternoon in the sunny warmth of a garden party surrounded by friends and ice-cold martinis, then hopped a bus for Toronto. When I arrived home early Sunday evening there was no one around. As so often after a public appearance, a party and a few drinks, I felt depleted and empty. I also felt aimless, not just about what I would do the rest of the evening but about what I would do and where I was really going with the rest of my life. Above all, I felt lonely. I was thirty-four.

In that mood, and with a suspicion that I was taking a dangerous and risky step, I made a telephone call to a young woman named Denise, whom I had known socially for several years. She was about my age, a Catholic, divorced, and attractive. She was a generous, thoughtful woman and was fun to be with. About fifteen minutes after my call, I ended up in her apartment and about an hour after that in her bed. It was my first attempt at making love and was loaded with anxiety because I feared that Denise might become pregnant. However, it was the beginning of a liaison that would last off and on for more than a decade.

It would be easy to say that this first experience with Denise, which was a serious violation of my vow of chastity, was a turning point, perhaps a fatal one in my spiritual journey as a Jesuit. But I believe this interpretation is too superficial. What happened in Denise's apartment that Sunday evening was, in my opinion, a symptom - a dramatic one - of a more profound spiritual malaise. It was not so much that through neglect and indifference my spiritual foundation as a Jesuit was crumbling. The truth was more stark. Whatever spiritual foundation I had laid down had been built upon shifting sand - another scriptural allusion that was always powerful and scary for me. And try as I might, I couldn't convert the sand into rock.

It wasn't that I didn't try. I prayed by the hour. I examined my conscience. I made retreats. I consulted spiritual directors and saw a psychiatrist. I read spiritual books, made visits to the chapel, read the office, said the rosary, made the stations of the cross and prayed for help daily at mass. The problem was that these spiritual activities never entered my bloodstream. For me they weren't real. It was like spending one's life reading the notes of a symphony but never making any music. I no more connected with Jesuit spirituality than I connected with my father. Nor do I believe one can grow spiritually unless one is growing emotionally. I did not grow emotionally in the Jesuits.

It was not surprising that the relationship with Denise, while it had periods of happiness and pleasure, was a disruptive, even a destructive one for both of us, often punctuated with angry outbursts and fuelled increasingly by alcohol. We were both looking for something that the other couldn't give. You can't give what you don't have. Which is why, although I favour optional celibacy, I don't think obligatory celibacy is the big problem in the Catholic priesthood. Lack of emotional maturity is. My guess is that many priests who have problems with celibacy would also have problems with marriage.

In June of 1958, I found it a relief to fly into New York to begin my stint as a summer editor on *America,* the current affairs weekly review staffed by American Jesuits. Headquarters for *America,* and living quarters for its staff, was Campion House, about two doors from where Irving Berlin had lived, a stone's throw from Riverside Drive just below Columbia University. Sometimes when I was sitting around the editorial table with these articulate and learned Jesuits, I had to pinch myself to see if I was dreaming. Yet these men always gave an attentive hearing to my suggestions, which were mostly about Canadian politics. (John Diefenbaker was then riding tall in the saddle.)

Thursday afternoon was our holiday. Three other Jesuit editors were avid golfers and needed a fourth so they dragooned me. I had never played golf in my life but they rustled me up some clubs. I might as well have been using hockey sticks. Nevertheless, every Thursday afternoon I was out there in New Jersey near Saddle River not far from President Nixon's home, hacking away at the fairways as though I was still coiling hay on Joe Gorman's farm. Sometimes I was half dead from insomnia but I still enjoyed the post-game ravioli dinners washed down by frosty American beer.

There was also a down side to my time at *America.* First, I was often conscious of a feeling of inferiority, of being "less than" this elite group of Jesuits, each of whom had made himself an expert in some field. Their articles emerged from an inner depth. Mine did not. I rummaged around in *The New York Times* or *The Globe and Mail,* clipped an item that caught my attention, then tried to construct a presentable commentary around it. Usually this system worked reasonably well. The real problem lay deeper. Looking back, I don't think I had much that I really wanted to say.

My second problem in New York was the old bugaboo, loneliness. I had no friends in the city and made none. All the other editors, some of whom had been on the staff for fifteen years, had their own circle of friends. They didn't introduce me to them. In fact, during the months I was living at *America*, I scarcely ever remember being invited into another Jesuit's room. To compensate for this feeling of isolation, I tramped the streets of upper Manhattan in the evenings, usually in Harlem, just a few blocks from Campion House. I think what attracted me to Harlem was its atmosphere of slight danger tinged with sexuality. I was always dressed in a black clerical suit with Roman collar. The streets teemed with people. Luscious young black women waved from hot fire escapes. Fruit vendors squeezed ripe oranges in the warm silky evening filled with people laughing, the scene colourful, earthy and electric.

In all the hours I tramped through Harlem, I was never in any trouble. One night a police cruiser stopped beside me and the officer told me I should go home. I did - but returned the next night. Some years later, in the summer of 1964, I was back in Harlem the night the trouble started - the fires, the fighting, the barricades and the police. I immediately telephoned *The Globe and Mail* and asked an editor if he wanted a story. I went back to *America*, wrote it, sent it by telegraph, and it appeared on the editorial page of the *Globe* a day later, evoking memories of those days so long ago in Hastings when I would send my stories to *The Peterborough Examiner* on the late night train.

9

SUICIDE AND ASYLUM

At the end of my first summer at *America,* August 1958, I flew to Cleveland to begin my final year of Jesuit training called tertianship. As the name suggests, tertianship was a kind of elevated third year novitiate or as St. Ignatius termed it, "the school of the heart." Should one's first fervour in the spiritual life have grown cold during the busy years of activity and study, tertianship was designed to rekindle it. The theory was that a spiritual fire would be lit under me and about thirty other tertians, mostly Americans, in the Jesuit tertianship located in Parma, a bourgeois suburb of Cleveland.

The schedule and content of the tertianship resembled that of the novitiate - prayer, work, study, and recreation. The studies focused on the Institute and traditions of the Society of Jesus, the core of Ignatian spirituality. As in the novitiate, the year began with a thirty-day long retreat in silence, then daily conferences on Jesuit spirituality given by the tertian master, Robert Walls. Not to put too fine a point on it, as a tertian master, Robert Walls was a bust. This was not my view alone but one shared by almost all the other tertians.

This raises an interesting question. Why did an organization as tightly structured and highly academic as the Jesuits keep jamming so many square pegs into so many round holes? It was not just Leo Nelligan in Guelph or Robert Walls in Parma. If I had wanted to raise one issue with the English Canadian province of the Society of Jesus as I knew it in mid-century, it would have been to question the high proportion of inadequate superiors who stayed in office interminably - the normal term was three years, usually renewed - swimming around in each other's bath water. The situation could not be blamed on lack of information. Jesuit headquarters in Rome had more information on their men than the CIA had on theirs.

True enough, the Upper Canadian English province of the Society of Jesus had only become autonomous in 1924 when it split from the French-Canadian province. Perhaps there had simply not been enough time to develop a strong cadre of superior personnel. There were exceptions, of course, but too many superiors played it safe until it was time for them to be re-appointed or transferred to another official position somewhere else. And some appointees were just plain inept.

I am afraid no other word will do for Father Walls and the kind of tertianship he ran in Parma. Far from being a "school of the heart" and the summit of Ignatian prayer, it was a spiritual desert marked by the occasional skirmish between the tertians and their master. Whatever his personal spiritual life - and I believe Father Walls was a kindly, if stubborn man, trying to do his level best - the master ran his tertianship the way Queeg ran his ship. Of course it didn't work. Some of the tertians were extremely bright, rightfully boasting about their own post-graduate degrees in theology and philosophy. During question period in the conferences on the Institute, these tertians nailed the master on mistakes, contradictions, non-sequiturs, cul-de-sacs, and positions that were indefensible. Nailing Father Walls was like shooting the light out of a sanctuary lamp at point-blank range, and eventually the tertians lost interest and gave up the sport. Sadly, the tertian master had lost our respect and from then on it was pretty much a matter of running out the clock.

Breaks from the deadly routine were provided by "experiments," designed to prepare us for our future priestly ministry. In the fall I went to Youngstown, Ohio, to spend a month as assistant chaplain in a Catholic hospital - a ministry that, despite my chronic insomnia, I liked better than any other. There was the satisfaction of quickly making friends with so many patients and the enjoyment of teamwork with the nurses and doctors. The sudden calls to emergency were also exciting. Once I gave the last rites to a Youngstown mobster who had been shot in the neck and was D.O.A.

Lent was the time for the major experiments. I was sent to give a mission in the Jesuit parish in Winnipeg and to the Ascension parish in Westmount, Quebec. I remember the long train ride across the wintry landscape to Manitoba - an anxious time because of my lack of sleep. I was warmly welcomed in Winnipeg in the Jesuit rectory at St. Ignatius by the pastor, Father Shaughnessy, a tall lumbering happy-go-lucky man whose heart was as big as his house. An older friendly Jesuit and I shared the mission. I had prepared a series of sermons in Cleveland mostly on such subjects as the "four last things" - death, judgement, heaven, and hell - at the time some of the staples of Jesuit missions. It seems ironic, but I expect some of my sermons on the eternity of hell were not unlike those Redemptorist sermons that had put the fear of God into me as a little boy in Hastings. One night, just as I was waxing eloquent on the terrible heat that melted ball bearings in hell forever, all the hot water radiators in the church began to rattle in unison.

It was toward the end of the second week that my own emotional radiator boiled over. I started my day at six in the morning, said mass for a congregation, preached several times during the day, spent hours in the confessional box, and led evening devotions. I did all this on little sleep, and on top of a growing anxiety suppressed by several stiff drinks of scotch around the kitchen table late at night. This was a recipe for serious trouble. I started to think more and more about suicide. I took my thoughts and troubles to Father Shaughnessy who was quite concerned. He suggested I speak to my old friend and mentor, Father George, now the new provincial, who happened to be in Winnipeg. Father George was equally concerned. The issue was whether I should go on to Montreal to give two more missions or cut my Lenten ministry short in Winnipeg. Father George thought it would be preferable for me to go to Montreal but to keep in close touch. I agreed and headed east.

It was the wrong decision. Montreal was a nightmare. The schedule for the missions in Ascension parish in the wealthy enclave of Westmount was about the same as in Winnipeg - mass, sermons, confessions, devotions, counselling. The difference was my Jesuit companion. John McCarthy, sometimes known as "Big Black John," was a large man with a voice that rumbled around the church like approaching thunder. He was a bluff American Irishman with a mean streak and a short fuse. Shortly after the mission began, I asked him if we could slightly modify the method for giving out communion at mass. Big John's fists clenched, his shoulders shook, his face became suffused with a fiery glow. He inhaled deeply from his ample diaphragm and let out a blood-curdling indictment of young whipper-snappers still wet behind the ears from the tertianship who thought they knew more than their betters. And I should know that my betters had been at this business since before I was born and had forgotten more in one day than I would pick up if I managed to live to be a hundred (which at that moment seemed improbable).

Then Big John tore off his mass vestments, brushed past me on his way out of the sacristy, sat down for breakfast, ordered two eggs boiled like hard balls, picked up the morning paper and never said another word. We had three days to go and I felt sick to my stomach. Some time after breakfast I knocked on Big John's door and apologized. It didn't do any harm, but it didn't do much good either. We would have virtually no further contact for the rest of the mission while we both preached the virtue of charity and the love of God as fervently as we could. I then did something I had never done before. I went out onto Sherbrooke Street in Westmount and bought a bottle of liquor, Black Velvet I think it was. For the next three days, especially before going to bed, I nursed that bottle like a baby. It helped dissolve the knot of anxiety and fear in my stomach. It was my friend.

After my final talk at the Ascension parish, I packed my bags, wrapping carefully what remained of the Black Velvet, flew to Toronto and saw Father Gordie George. He encouraged me to return to Cleveland and finish the tertianship. Later we would discuss the next step, perhaps a degree in history. A day later I was back in Parma, a little shaky from lack of sleep but determined to carry on as best I could. The tertian master, Father Walls, had a different idea. Naturally he had heard about my threats of suicide and just as naturally he was concerned. He convinced me to go into a local Catholic hospital, talk with a doctor and get some sleep. I did.

A fresh bed, friendly nurses, a strong sleeping potion and an upbeat doctor did wonders. I awoke in the morning to sunlight streaming across the fresh bed linens and a nurse bringing me hot tea. I was thoroughly refreshed and feeling like a new man. Father Walls came into the room, friendly and solicitous. I thought he had come to take me back to the tertianship. Little did I know. Next the young doctor appeared and said he wanted me to go to Detroit for further medical consultations. Father Walls backed him up. Initially, I objected, but all my life I have tended to defer to doctors. I deferred. So we drove back to the tertianship where I packed a small bag. "Just in case," Father Walls said, "you might have to stay overnight." To my surprise, one of my closest tertian friends, Bob Braus, a Korean War veteran from California, was waiting in the car. How kind of Father Walls, I thought, to invite Bob to come.

We arrived in Dearborn, on the outskirts of Detroit, before noon. In front of us I saw a red brick building, a block or so long and several stories high, fronted by acres of dead grass salted with dirty snow and surrounded by an ugly steel fence. We drove in through the gates and pulled up before a large portico. Accompanied by my two companions, I entered the reception area with a feeling of curiosity. I expected that I would have an interview, maybe a test for insomnia, and be back in Cleveland in time for supper.

Father Walls went into a small office, presumably to tell the receptionist we had arrived, while Bob and I chatted in the lounge. Then Father Walls returned and said there were some papers I should fill out while he and Bob went out to lunch. I sat down and began to fill out the papers which seemed innocuous enough to me. There was a lot of fine print which I didn't bother to read. The place was comfortably called St. Joseph's Retreat. There were several nuns floating around in white habits and I found their friendly faces reassuring.

But when I had signed my name to the last of the papers, it was not a smiling nun who came to take me to my next appointment. No indeed. Instead it was a large officious-looking muscular woman in a white uniform with enough keys at her waist to lock up Alcatraz. She extracted a long key from her belt and opened a locked door which I had not noticed before, just as I had not noticed the steel bars on all the windows. She then led me down a short hall, took out another key and opened another door which she carefully locked behind us. Suddenly I felt claustrophobic and began to panic.

"Where are we?" I demanded of my custodian. "Where are we going? And where in hell are my two Jesuit friends?" Her answer was curt and devastating. This was a Catholic mental institution. Further, she informed me, I had signed myself into an asylum and my Jesuit friends had gone back to Cleveland. I think the information that my friends had abandoned me made me more angry than the realization I was locked up in a nut house and that my muscular guide had suddenly become my jailer.

I started to rant and rave: "There's nothing the matter with me! I want to get out of here this minute! And if you don't let me go, I'll call my lawyer and sue the Archdiocese of Detroit!" Never mind I had never had a lawyer in my life and had no clue how to retain one. My ranting drew some mild attention from other people, all men, walking around in white smocks, presumably now my fellow inmates. When I was a little kid in Hastings, I had heard about a place in Whitby where they knocked some people out with electric shocks and kept plunging other people into ice-cold water. Was that to be my fate behind the next locked door?

My new jailer ignored my rage and my threats. Instead she summoned two men in white coats who escorted me to a small neat bedroom, asked me to take off all my clothes, then left, taking my overnight bag with them. I sat on the bed, took stock of my situation and concluded my choices were limited. My Jesuit colleagues were halfway back to Cleveland. Apparently I had signed myself into a locked asylum and I didn't have a key.

So I took off my clothes and was sitting starkers on the bed when the two orderlies returned. One handed me a package with not much more than my toothbrush in it. The other gave me a white gown resembling a cheap bathrobe. I asked if I could have my cigarettes. Years ago in philosophy days, I had convinced a doctor to prescribe six cigarettes a day for my nerves and I had been unilaterally increasing the dosage ever since. The one orderly explained that I could not keep any cigarettes but they would be doled out upon request. What about my cigarette lighter? There was a communal lighter hanging from a chain in the recreation room. And with that helpful information they disappeared again.

Now in my very own white coat, I ventured out into what seemed a spacious lounge-recreation room with men of various ages sitting, reading, smoking, chatting, playing table tennis, and watching television with the volume turned too high. I chatted with several younger people who looked the brightest - not always a sure test - and learned that the most serious cases were on the top floor. As an inmate's sanity returned or improved, he would gradually work his way down to the ground floor where we were. This was a comforting thought. I asked for a cigarette, lit it from the lighter hanging from the chain, took a satisfying drag, and, somewhat to my consternation, started to feel better.

I couldn't believe how soundly I slept the first night in the asylum. I awoke refreshed, ate a hearty breakfast of bacon and eggs and waited for the next development. I didn't have to wait long. A doctor, not a psychiatrist, came into my room, asked me a few questions, then told me I could have outside privileges. This meant I could come and go pretty much as I pleased, although I had to be inside the asylum by nine o'clock. I felt I had just been awarded the Victoria Cross. There was one catch. I was the only one in the group who had these privileges, so

I had to take orders for anything the other guys wanted from outside the steel fence - magazines, candies, cigarettes, newspapers, things like that. I felt as though I was running a smuggling operation. I also felt special - like the time I won the oratorical contest or spoke at a first mass or was assigned to *America*. Even though I was only a one-eyed leader in the kingdom of the blind, it was the feeling that counted.

I remained at the asylum, or more pleasantly, St. Joseph's Retreat, for almost three weeks. They were relaxed weeks - no pressure, no superiors, no duties or obligations except to act as a runner for my fellow inmates. I was a chief with a few followers and no real duties. Several times, for brief periods, I would see a psychiatrist with whom I did not get on. I believe he felt I was slightly nuts and the feeling was reciprocated. One morning, with a couple of aides, he came sweeping into my room. About fifty years old, brisk, no beating around the bush, he asked me a couple of questions, then stooped down and peered at me more closely. Forty years later I remember exactly what he said: "If you pulled up your socks and got off your ass, I think you'd be fine." Then he wheeled around, strode out of the room, and I never saw him again.

Three weeks after my induction in Dearborn, Father Walls and Bob Braus came to take me back to Cleveland. I was happy to see them. There were no recriminations. When we got back, Father Walls did his level best to find psychological support for me. He also very kindly told me to take it easy for the final six weeks and follow only as much of the program as I wished. That suited me fine. Again I was special, and made all my fellow tertians envious. Moreover, Father Walls never even mentioned another of my transgressions. Some weeks before my incarceration in the asylum, I had arranged, against all the rules, for *The Cleveland Plain Dealer* to be delivered every morning. The paper boy was to wrap it carefully and leave it in a drain pipe on the edge of the grounds. Unfortunately, when I went to Detroit expecting to return immediately, I had said nothing to the paper boy, who kept jamming *Plain Dealers* into the drain pipe until water began to flood back into the vegetable cellar. It was an apt metaphor for my tertianship - all clogged up.

10

WEALTHY WIDOWS AND SPEAKERS' CORNER

In June 1959, back in Toronto, my fifteen-year training period at an end, my spiritual life at low ebb, I waited at the old Jesuit Seminary for my first assignment which I expected would be further studies in Canadian history at the University of Toronto. Imagine my surprise when the seminary rector, Father Ed Sheridan, casually introduced the possibility of my spending a year raising money. The Jesuits had finally decided to abandon the draughty seminary the Loretto Sisters had foisted upon them twenty-five years before and were to build a modern theologate in the Bayview district of North Toronto. This required money, a lot of money, and before going to Cleveland, some other scholastics and I had been remarkably successful in raising some of it.

So my reaction to the idea of spending a year raising funds was positive. This would give me freedom, excitement and a special status. I made only one request, that my good Jesuit friend, Howard Logan would join me. "Logie," as we usually called him, had a big girth and a big heart. He was addicted to cigarettes, paperback books and the stock market. Logie was in charge of the Jesuit investment portfolio and followed the market the way a sports junkie follows the scores. "I think gold is breaking loose," he would say, lighting a filter cigarette, before he said good morning. I thought we might make a good team. So did our superiors. They gave us the green light for a year of fund raising to help finish the new seminary. It was a risk. But we had no money to lose and we might make some.

Fortunately we made quite a lot of money, partly by following the simple advice of a successful Toronto businessman: approach widows who have control of their own estates. I still remember the night in Rosedale when I knocked on the door, was let in by the

97

maid, and sat down in the drawing room to talk money with an impeccably dressed widow in her early sixties. We had a pleasant chat, she agreed it was a worthy cause (she had many Jesuit friends), went to her desk and wrote a cheque which she put in a sealed envelope just before we said good-bye. So as not to seem too eager, I drove my car a couple of blocks before I stopped, turned on the light, tore open the envelope and read the amount - $25,000.

Every time Logie and I made a killing, we treated ourselves to dinner at the Rathskeller room of the Walker House, usually wiener schnitzel washed down with quarts of German beer. Eventually we collected about $300,000 - enough to complete the new seminary as originally designed. It had been a relatively happy and productive year for me. Even the insomnia was better, probably because I had easier access to sleeping pills and was taking more of them. I was still seeing my psychiatrist, Dr. Bremner, for my neuroses and Denise for my love life. I managed to avoid serious questions about the hypocrisy of this or whether my life had any meaning.

So far as I knew, after a summer holiday and our annual eight-day retreat, I would resume my history courses at the University of Toronto. It was not to be. In early July my provincial, Gordie George, summoned me to his residence in Rosedale to ask whether I would like to join a small group of Jesuits in London, England, who were launching a new spiritual periodical to be called *The Way*. The Canadian Jesuit they had requested, an expert in ascetical theology, was unable to go. I had no special expertise in this area but Father George thought I could help. Looking back now, I think he was trying to give me a break with a period of stimulating work outside the country. I quickly calculated this was another prestige assignment with a trip overseas to boot, so I accepted.

Father Logie was going to St. Beuno's in Wales to do his own year of tertianship. In August we left from New York on the *Nieuw Amsterdam* for a champagne crossing to Southampton. I took the boat-train to London where a hilarious Cockney taxi driver dropped me off in the heart of Mayfair at the famous Jesuit residence, Farm Street. This house has appeared in many English novels including Evelyn Waugh's *Brideshead Revisited*. Draw a line from Speakers' Corner in Hyde Park near Marble Arch through to Berkeley Square, and you will find Farm Street about in the middle, kitty-corner from the Connaught Hotel. A large double house also fronting on Duke Street, Farm Street had a reputation for catering to upper-crust English Catholics.

So it was with trepidation that I rang the doorbell of perhaps the most famous Jesuit residence in the English-speaking world. A lay brother answered the door and peered at me suspiciously. Most ordinary people, including ordinary Jesuits, were not welcome at Farm Street. He reluctantly showed me into a gloomy parlour where, after a nervous wait, I finally met the man I would be working for. Father Philip Caraman was about forty-three, a short, slight Jesuit of Lebanese descent, with a darting smile and a sallow complexion. He had the reputation of asking simple questions to which there were no simple answers. He had written several spiritual biographies, edited more than one respected journal and did not suffer fools at all. Caraman had a coterie of aristocratic and literary friends that included Alec Guinness, Graham Greene and Evelyn Waugh. When I was at Farm Street, Waugh's much beloved daughter, Margaret, worked for Caraman. Tragically, she died in a motor accident in London in 1986.

Caraman had two associates on the projects he was directing. James Walsh was a gentle unassuming Jesuit with a quick brain and a finely modulated sense of humour. William Yeoman, in his early thirties the youngest of the three, was built like a football halfback, liked good food and better wine, was bright and knew it. So this was the Jesuit trio with whom I had, willy-nilly, thrown in my lot for a year. At the beginning we got on fine. I attended discussions on designing the new magazine, *The Way*, often at night over a bottle of scotch in Caraman's quarters. But presently the cordial atmosphere began to change and for a simple reason. The Farm Street trio had concluded, and with good cause, that I had neither the knowledge of spirituality nor the language skills to deliver what they needed.

But Philip Caraman was not an unkindly or thoughtless man. He made a final effort to pull me back onto the team by asking me to fly to Holland with him where we would negotiate a contract to print *The Way*. The first copy was due out in the spring of 1961. After we had signed the contract, Caraman generously suggested I stay over for a short holiday in the Jesuit residence near Queen Wilhelmina's palace. I spent the time sight-seeing - the house where Anne Frank had lived, some art galleries and a boat trip. But

I also decided one dark October night to tour the red-light district and have a look at the ladies in the windows, the famous Amsterdam prostitutes. I was wearing my Roman collar covered by a scarf. Unfortunately, a drunken Finnish sailor accosted me as I was crossing a canal, smashed me in the face, broke my glasses and left me bleeding on the cobblestones. The police took care of the drunken sailor, a young Jesuit-trained doctor took care of my eye, and the story of an innocent Canadian Jesuit being attacked made the front page of several Dutch newspapers. Only the communist paper raised the question of what I might be doing in the red-light district so late at night.

Of course, the fracas in Amsterdam did nothing to resolve my growing alienation at Farm Street. Caraman and his associates soon began to ignore me. What made the climate even more uncomfortable was that I became caught in the cross fire between Caraman's trying to build a literary empire on one side of the house and the Jesuit superior, Thomas Corbishely - later the first Roman Catholic priest to speak in Westminster Abbey since the reformation - trying to protect his turf on the other side of the house.

Fuelled by what I perceived to be rejection on all sides, my problem with loneliness increased as did my insomnia. Fortunately, I found a kindly doctor at Farm Street who thought it was better to sleep than not to sleep. He gave me a supply of my old friends, the Seconals. To cope with the loneliness, I tramped the streets of London - in my view, far and away the most interesting city I've ever been in - snaffled a scarce ticket to watch Queen Elizabeth open Parliament, took some voice training from the actor and writer Robert Speaight, and went backstage to have tea with Paul Scofield after watching his mesmerizing performance as Thomas More in *A Man For all Seasons*. I also enjoyed many chats with the famous Jesuit Archbishop Roberts, who lived at Farm Street and who had been refused entry to the United States because of his anti-nuclear activities. I drank port with Farm Street's many interesting guests, such as the Oxford philosopher and well-known atheist, A.J. Ayer.

But despite London's many allures, my favourite spot was Speakers' Corner in Hyde Park, a five-minute walk from Farm Street just up from the Dorchester Hotel near Marble Arch. Every

100

Sunday after lunch I would stroll over and never tired of the cacophony of voices emanating from orators black, brown, white and yellow - men and women from all parts of the world praising anarchy, denouncing democracy, extolling Marxism and free love and abolishing the monarchy, advocating abortion, praying the rosary, and castigating the Pope. This bellowing brew of banter, hectoring, oratory, heckling, sarcasm, and hoots of laughter I never failed to find enormously entertaining.

I remember the head of the Methodist Church on his little wooden soapbox preaching God's word, rain or shine. Twenty years later I would go back and he would still be there, now Lord Soper, in his eighties, newly appointed by the Queen to the House of Lords. Frank Sheed and Maisie Ward, the Catholic apologists and publishers, were sometimes there, as were speakers from atheists to zealots and most everyone in between. It was a melange whose bellicosity was only exceeded by its good humour. Gradually I summoned enough nerve to begin heckling various speakers, especially the communists. I became known as "the colonial." I always planned to take a little chair and start ranting about something or other but I never did and I still regret it.

As Christmas approached and holiday lights lit up Oxford and Regent Streets, my feelings of rejection and loneliness coalesced into a leaden lump in my gut. These feelings were only briefly relieved, on Christmas Eve, by going to help the chaplain at Brize Norton, a NATO air base in the Cotswolds, about an hour from London. Security at the base was heavy and so was the paradox in celebrating the birthday of the Prince of Peace while driving by squadrons of aircraft loaded with atomic warheads.

When I returned to a deserted Farm Street early on the afternoon of Christmas Day, loneliness swept over me like the cold English rain. For a few desolate moments I stared out the streaky window towards Berkeley Square. Then I did what I had done some years before in Toronto. I telephoned a woman friend. Her name was Julie. She was on Caraman's staff and I had worked with her on correspondence. "By all means," she responded warmly, "come on out and have Christmas dinner with my family in Wimbledon." I shaved and began to feel better.

Julie was nineteen, a slight, attractive girl who resembled a young Audrey Hepburn. Gradually her home at Wimbledon became a refuge for me and I went there with increasing frequency, as indeed I began to seek out Julie's company more often at Farm Street. Perhaps with few interests, no real friends and little focus to my own life, it was inevitable that my loneliness became transformed into an infatuation with Julie. After work we walked for miles through London's lovely parks, chattering away like two teenagers until it was time for her to take the tube to Wimbledon. One afternoon we had high tea at the Ritz. It was also inevitable that this relationship would be noticed and it was. Father Caraman ordered me to stop working with Julie. Her mother became concerned.

To no avail. Our emotional infatuation continued more intensely than ever. It came to a new pitch one lovely sunny Sunday when we had arranged to meet at Kew Gardens and then take a bus to Hampton Court. After a late tea we sat on the warm grass and began to play around in a fairly innocent fashion. But innocent or not, I think we both suddenly realized we were on the edge of a precipice. We picked up our belongings and took the bus back to London. I was shocked and upset, so much so that I immediately arranged to take an early-morning train to the Jesuit tertianship at St. Beuno's in Wales. I wanted to discuss what had happened with the tertian master, Father Paul Kennedy, and ask him to direct me in a retreat.

Father Kennedy was in his sixties, a rumpled, untidy man, a heavy smoker whose last meal you could deduce by looking at the stains on the front of his cassock. He was also one of the most perceptive spiritual directors I ever encountered. I don't remember all that much about the content of the retreat he gave me when I visited him three or four times a day for spiritual direction. I do remember he insisted on strenuous physical exercise, so I spent most of my afternoons climbing the lovely Welsh hills where I could see across to Mount Snowdon. And I remember feeling reasonably serene on the train ride back from Wales, looking at the picturesque thatched cottages, resolved that the relationship with Julie must end.

It didn't. Instead, we continued our walks and our trysts until it was time for me to leave Farm Street in mid-June 1961. My plan was to return home with stops in Rome, Portugal and Spain. Despite her mother's wishes to the contrary, Julie came to Heathrow to see me off. There were tears, promises, hugs and a high quotient of mush.

The two weeks in Rome were a washout. Of course the problem wasn't Rome - it was me. Or to use my favourite Latin aphorism: *quidquid recipitur per modum recipientis recipitur*, which is to say, "If you take a signet ring and impress it on a pound of steel, then on a pound of butter, the resulting imprint depends upon the recipient, not on the signet ring." So the soft ochre light suffusing the hills of Rome at sunset was discoloured by the prism of my own emotions, grim, grey and humourless. I felt angry and resentful toward Farm Street, sentimental and sad about Julie, apprehensive and confused about my future.

So Rome was a grey smear. I looked at the streets crawling with priests and monks in musty cassocks. They looked like black beetles. I had an image again and again of the Church as a bloated structure, top-heavy with oppressive authority. The image did not change when I went to St. Peter's for a public audience with the man at the top of the bureaucracy, Pope John XXIII. I consider him a great Pope. But as I watched him being carried in pomp and pageantry into St. Peter's, I had no feeling of awe or admiration. In fact, I had been more moved when I saw the Queen open Parliament. Of course, feelings don't have much to do with faith. Still, even now, thirty-five years later, I have no desire to return to Rome.

My plan was to go home via Spain so I could see some of the famous shrines associated with the founder of the Jesuits, St. Ignatius. But as my departure date approached, I became more and more frantic. I was tired, sleepless, lonely and confused. I seemed to be splitting apart, a feeling that William James called "torn-to-pieces-hood," his succinct transliteration of the German *Zerrissenheit*. I was like a frightened bird trapped in an empty house desperately trying to get out, becoming more fatigued and frantic with every failed effort to escape. I telephoned the airlines, changed my flights, then telephoned again and changed them back. The way I was feeling, a pilgrimage to Spain to see Ignatian shrines made about as much sense as an invalid signing on to run the marathon. Finally, I summoned all the energy I had left, changed my ticket to a direct flight to New York and prayed to God that my dear friends from Kingston days, Jean and Maurice O'Connor, would be home.

As the aircraft rose over Rome I began to relax. The frenzy subsided. The ice cube inside me began to melt. Because of the time change, by mid-afternoon I was in the town of Ossining (with its infamous prison) in Westchester County, about an hour's drive north of New York City. Several years before, Maurice O'Connor had left Kingston with his family to become one of the directors of an exclusive psychiatric clinic on a large estate overlooking the Hudson River in Ossining. Jean greeted me with a smile and a hug and we sat in their sunny living room with a cold drink and began to catch up. It was like being in a warm emotional bath - safe, secure, loved. I lit a cigarette, took a deep satisfying breath and began to live again.

About five o'clock, Maurice strolled over from his office and we went out into the back yard for a chat. In many ways Maurice was as laconic as Jean was loquacious. He had a depth and insight that I sometimes found intimidating. (I think he was on the cutting edge of his profession in his analysis of the nature of schizophrenia.) Whenever I played bridge with Maurice, not often and not well, I had the impression he possessed a kind of X-ray vision by which he knew every card in my hand. Although he was my friend, not my psychiatrist, I sometimes felt he saw through me the way he saw through my cards.

Maurice asked me what had happened at Farm Street. I told him and he said simply, "You blew it." He then asked, with just a note of mild frustration, why had I not seized other opportunities, perhaps touring Europe, when I realized Farm Street was not working out. I had no answer. We then talked briefly about what I should do next. Should I resume the study of history? Maurice didn't think it mattered all that much what I did so long as I didn't throw in the towel again as I had in Farm Street. And whatever I did, he insisted, should stretch me. Then it was time for drinks, as always a double martini with an olive for me, and dinner. I remember dinner because we went out to an elegant restaurant where I saw alligator meat on the menu for the first and only time.

11

BOOKS AND BOOZE

After ten days with the O'Connors in Ossining, I returned to Toronto revived and refreshed. But I sensed the feeling was only temporary, that sooner or later the snarling dogs below - the anger, the anxiety, the fear - would return. After a talk with the Jesuit provincial, Gordie George, it was decided that I would go on for an M.A. in Canadian history at the University of Toronto. Although more Jesuits were now being sent for graduate studies, I still considered this assignment a plum. There was a time when the Jesuits thought that their own course of studies was more than adequate and further courses in secular universities were superfluous. Father Eric O'Connor, who had completed a splendid doctorate in mathematics at Harvard and helped start the highly respected Thomas More Institute in Montreal, had changed that attitude. So had Father Bernard Lonergan from Buckingham, Quebec, a theological scholar of international repute.

For me, at any rate, studies at Toronto were preferable to teaching in a dusty classroom in Regina. I moved into the Jesuit university residence, a large comfortable red brick house at 226 St. George Street, a few tree-lined blocks above Bloor Street in what is called the Annex. Denise came back into my life with her generous support and affection, most of our visits accompanied by liberal doses of alcohol.

My two years, September 1961 until June 1963, studying history in Toronto were relatively happy ones. The Jesuit community, mostly university students at 226 St. George, was pleasant and I got on well with the superior, Father Oliver. I liked the work in history, especially the seminars, and enjoyed the company of my fellow students, some of whom would go on to distinguished careers - John Reid as federal cabinet minister, Jack Granatstein and Irving Abella as prominent Canadian historians, my good friend Rick Alway as warden of Hart House and later the first lay president of St. Michael's College, and the irrepressible Larry Zolf to become beached at the CBC.

My thesis director, Jack Saywell, was a young creative and enthusiastic historian who introduced us to prominent French-Canadians such as André Laurendeau. My thesis was on the Ontario provincial election of 1934 which brought the flamboyant Mitch Hepburn and the Liberals to power. The thesis defense began in the history department with Saywell and several other professors, but presently we all adjourned and continued the defense at a well-known Greek tavern on lower Yonge Street.

So I earned my M.A. in Canadian history and was planning to receive it formally at the University convocation to be held on November 22, 1963. At one o'clock I visited my dentist, then walked back to 226, arriving just after two. Immediately I noticed a group of Jesuits around the television set. I looked at the screen in horror and disbelief as a shaken Walter Cronkite announced that President Kennedy had just been assassinated. I did not attend my graduation ceremony.

After I had obtained my M.A. in history, to my astonishment, Father George asked if I would be interested in doing a second graduate degree in Communication Arts. I suspect he had two reasons for this proposal: Loyola College in Montreal was introducing a communications department and a double degree would be valuable for teaching there; secondly, Father George knew of my interest in radio and television and no doubt felt this would be engrossing for me. Needless to say, I jumped at the opportunity and so began another M.A., this time at the University of Michigan in Ann Arbor in September 1963.

The two years I spent at Ann Arbor were the happiest of my Jesuit career. Not because of any fervour in my spiritual life - which I had pretty well dropped. I no longer meditated or even said mass on a regular basis. All this had long since lost its savour. Life in Ann Arbor was quite a different matter. It was a lovely university city which some novelists have used as a setting in their fiction. We boarded in private houses, ate some meals in the hospital cafeteria and the rest at one of the German restaurants downtown where we had spicy fat sausages smothered in hot mustard, washed down with golden pitchers of ice-cold beer. Occasionally we would then repair to the Pretzel Bell, the university pub, where we engaged in chug-a-lugs, standing on a table gulping as much beer as possible in the shortest time without choking. Our group of priests, mostly Jesuits studying for advanced degrees, also had our own parties where drinks were poured with a heavy hand and I had more than my share of double manhattans and frosty martinis.

What made my two years at Ann Arbor particularly stimulating were my communications courses. These were, for the most part, hands-on classes held in the impressive radio and television studios of the University. We became as familiar with microphones as with our electric razors. We did everything in a TV studio from swinging the boom to interviewing the guests to writing scripts, and we did it all with an air of professionalism. I got on well with my fellow students, all much younger, and with my professors. In fact, I did not have much difficulty obtaining my Master's degree at Michigan and took the view that the project was not too demanding. My best friend, Bob Maloney from California, and others were more generous. They said I didn't find the work difficult because I was good at it. Maybe they were right.

Describing the University of Michigan without mentioning football would be like visiting the Vatican without referring to the Sistine Chapel. When I was there, the Wolverines were one of the best college football teams in the United States, and they still are. The football stadium at Ann Arbor seats 105,000 people. Imagine a warm, bright October afternoon, the leaves turning to garnet and gold, the air electric with students chanting the school songs, the stadium packed with colourful groups of fans looking like patches of bright flowers. Michigan's hundred-strong marching band in their blue and gold uniforms fills the autumn air with music stirring enough to raise the hair on the back of your head.

Michigan is playing Michigan State. It is the fourth quarter, minutes to go. Michigan State needs a touchdown to win. Suddenly as the sun begins to sink behind the stadium, Michigan State's quarterback falls back and unleashes a forty-yard pass that floats and floats in the crisp air. The ball begins to descend in a graceful arc toward the Michigan goal line, where at the last second the Michigan State receiver lunges forward, stretches flat out and strains for the ball. It just misses his fingertips. He falls to the ground. The crowd explodes. The victorious music of Michigan's marching band bounces from the vault of the crimson sky. It's good to be there. It's good to be with friends. It's good to be alive.

Finally, on a clear sunny morning in June, I got into my rented car, said good-bye to Bob Maloney and left Ann Arbor. I left with good memories, such as the time on Good Friday afternoon when I went by myself to the University's main auditorium to hear Billy Graham preach. I don't know what had moved me to go. I think somewhere in my Catholic soul I still dimly believed that Protestants would get into a lot of trouble if they didn't shape up and become Catholics before it was too late. So I was surprised when I heard Billy Graham speak for an hour on the Passion of Christ, and found myself moved spiritually in a way I had not been moved for a long time. Other memories stand out, such as the afternoon I stood and cheered and punched the air when a Canadian horse named Northern Dancer won the Kentucky Derby, and those Sunday nights when I invited my American Jesuit friends over to my place to watch the CBC's presentation of *This Hour has Seven Days*, and enjoyed their chagrin when they realized they didn't have anything to match it.

I did not go back to Ann Arbor for my graduation when President Lyndon Johnson gave his "Great Society" speech. After returning to Toronto in early June, I wondered how much longer I could avoid teaching in the classroom. Come to think of it, I am not sure it was the classroom - where I had been a fairly effective teacher - that I wanted to avoid so much as the kind of Jesuit school community life that I had found so stultifying and enervating. Still, I did make a final effort to stay out of the schools. I dug out my 400-page thesis and hawked it around to various publishers. Only one, the dynamic and irrepressible Jack McClelland, was enthusiastic. He thought a biography of Mitch Hepburn, Premier of Ontario at Queen's Park from 1934 to 1942, with his flamboyant lifestyle (based in an opulent suite of Toronto's King Edward Hotel and paid for by his political friends), his heavy drinking and habitual womanizing, would make a sure-fire biography. Jack McClelland stood up, pumped my hand, gave me the thumbs up and said to go for it.

I went for it and sold the idea to Father George and my other superiors. I visited Mitch Hepburn's widow, still living on the family farm near St. Thomas. She was reluctant to cooperate in the project because of the shadow side of her husband's public career. However, I was to be more than gratified that by the time *Mitch Hepburn* was published, she and I were good friends. After a day's writing, I would often head downtown to my favourite bar at 300 College Street which had a musical trio with a fantastic trumpet player. I usually sat at a table alone, drinking beer, listening to the music, getting a quiet buzz on while I imagined ways of bringing Mitch Hepburn to life on paper.

Weekends I often spent with Denise reading the newspapers and drinking gin and tonic in her back yard, often with other friends. She was generous and good company. On the whole it was a pleasant regimen and the snarling dogs, still lurking beneath the surface, were pretty well leashed.

Finally, in October 1967, *Mitch Hepburn*, the first biography of the St. Thomas premier, was published to generally good reviews. I was especially pleased that the literary editor of *The Globe and Mail*, William French, made the Hepburn book the lead review in the paper's Saturday edition. There were only two severely negative reviews that I remember. One, in *The Toronto Telegram*, was by the CBC's factotum, Larry Zolf, who had done much valuable research on Hepburn and had also planned to write a biography. The University of Toronto newspaper, *The Varsity*, complained I had made no effort to prove that Hepburn was a fascist. Of course, I could not have done the Hepburn biography without the generosity and enthusiastic support of the Jesuit order, and we were all gratified when the book won the University of British Columbia Medal for the best Canadian biography in the Centennial Year.

Long before *Mitch Hepburn* was published, I knew I had a problem that was growing more serious, even dangerous. The problem was alcohol. I don't know whether or not I had a problem with alcohol from the beginning - although I well remember the beginning. I had been visiting friends in Toronto on Labour Day weekend, 1940. I was at a party the night before, had a lot of drinks with no realization of their strength or effect, got on a Toronto streetcar where I threw up all over my clothes, and had difficulty finding a dry cleaner open because of the holiday.

A few years later a friend and I joined a group in a restaurant in downtown Toronto to celebrate the end of our school year at St. Michael's College. I thought we were drinking ginger ale. In fact we were drinking ginger ale laced with rye in liberal quantities. The next thing I remember is waking up in front of the steps of the Parliament Buildings at Queen's Park early in the morning. In full view of the cars streaming up University Avenue, I staggered to my feet and proceeded to urinate all over the steps of the Parliament Buildings. Did I do this because my father was an alcoholic or because my "inner child" was writhing in pain or because the Conservatives had just come to power at Queen's Park? I don't know and I don't think the answer matters much. The fact is I was drunk and had suffered my first blackout.

Of course there was no drinking during the early years of Jesuit training. But eventually I began to socialize almost exclusively with friends who drank, and my relationship with Denise was saturated with alcohol. During my years at Ann Arbor, I would sometimes go into Detroit for the weekend, get a room at a cheap hotel and drink manhattans at a favourite bar that had shamrocks on the tables I always went alone but I never felt lonely. By this time alcohol had become my friend. It warmed and then melted the icy feeling of anxiety and fear in my stomach. For a time at least it bridged the split between the way I felt about myself and the way I wanted others to see me. Instead of being fragmented, I felt whole. The interior dis-ease began to subside. And in a curious way, though I sat at the shamrock tables drinking alone, I began to feel connected to others and the world outside in a way I had not before. Sometimes when I was drinking with a group of people, the alcohol put me in touch with the years of accumulated anger and, like my father, I became truculent and obnoxious.

It was about 1965, I think, that I began to drink on a daily basis and, more to the point, compulsively. Unlike ordinary social drinkers, I was never sure what would happen after the first drink. I might get pleasantly or obnoxiously drunk or I might not. Certainly I began to experience more blackouts. I would wake up in the morning not being sure what had happened the night before, what I had said or whom I had insulted. One night late, driving home to the provincial's residence in Rosedale, I side-swiped a portico just beneath his bedroom window, smashing one of the supporting columns and almost bringing the whole structure down on my head. Next morning at breakfast I pretended I knew nothing about it and the matter was not pressed.

But I could only pretend for so long although in a sense my whole life had been a pretense. The alcohol, while acting as an anaesthetic, only added another layer of unreality and deception. Gradually I began to admit I had a problem. But to my way of thinking the problem was not alcoholism, it was emotional and psychological. Through the years since the scared little boy crouched inside the bell jar on the steps of the hardware store in Hastings, the knot of fear and anxiety in the pit of my stomach had never really gone away. It had only hardened and become more imbedded. The snarling dogs were always there, leashed at times, but never giving up their effort to break loose and destroy. I had tried many strategies to keep the dogs at bay - becoming head altar boy, writing for Robertson Davies, earning success in school, joining the Jesuits (the Cadillacs of the Catholic priesthood), writing for prestigious magazines, and publishing an award-winning book, with all the plaudits that kind of success, temporary as it is, entails. Then there was the long and comfortable but ultimately destructive relationship with Denise, the sleeping pills, and the daily medication of booze requiring ever heavier dosages to make the anaesthetic work.

In the end, none of these bromides worked effectively and the inner dis-ease became more difficult to bear. I was feeling more and more uncomfortable in my skin - angry, anxious, aimless. My Jesuit superiors, hoping I would find my feet, had given me no definite assignments. Some of my friends, Jesuits and others, quietly expressed their concern about my drinking. So one day in April 1969, because I could see no alternative, I drove along St. John's side road north of Aurora through the rolling green horse country and turned in at a gate marked Southdown, a treatment centre supported by the Roman Catholic Archdiocese of Toronto. It was mainly for priests with addiction and other psychological problems.

I had an interview with the director in which he asked me to answer the famous Johns Hopkins twenty-question test designed for people with a probable drinking problem. Three positive answers, and chances were you were an alcoholic. I answered "Yes" to thirteen of the questions. So after discussing the problem with my provincial, Father Robert Macdougall, I reluctantly agreed to enter Southdown for treatment.

On May 5, 1969, after a couple of beers and lunch with Denise at the Colonnade restaurant on Bloor Street, I packed my bag and got into the car with my old friend, Father Howie Logan, who was driving me to Southdown. An incident happened on the way, the significance of which I only recognized much later. I suggested to Logie that we stop on the way and have a bloody mary. I don't think I even wanted a drink. In some curious way I was just trying to test my friend. Under the circumstances, Logie, quite rightly, declined. Whereupon, my anger and resentment turned to ice and I gave Logie the "Frigidaire treatment." I refused to speak to him. Even when he became lost, I would not give him the correct directions.

Fortunately Logie had a good sense of direction. He got back on track but he didn't go directly to Southdown. Instead he drove to a bar in Aurora. Even before I ordered a double rye and ginger I felt better. It wasn't so much that I needed the drink. It was more that I had regained control of the situation. It was only much later that I realized how much the need to control had affected my life and that of others, and what a price I paid trying to maintain it.

To my surprise I remained at Southdown for six months, twice the usual term. For me, Southdown, not unlike the asylum in Detroit, was a safe, secure and pleasant place. The rooms were spacious, the meals tasty and the staff supportive. Most days we were busy with group and individual therapy, physical exercise, walks in the surrounding woods and hills, friendly discussions and recreation. Almost immediately I began to feel better, more relaxed, more at ease. Many years later I realized at the experiential level that comfort and security, no matter how pleasant one's surroundings, must come from within not from without. The resident psychologist, Marc Eveson, had a special insight into the addictive personality and he suggested I spend a couple of hours a day writing about my life to see what underlying themes and patterns emerged. I found this a stimulating exercise resulting in, finally, about 400 typed pages.

I rather enjoyed the group therapy, which because of my verbal skills I often dominated, or more accurately, tried to control. This was about the time Marc Eveson asked me in one of our private sessions whether I really wanted (yet again) to be a one-eyed leader in the kingdom of the blind. I expect the answer was yes. I remember in group therapy getting into many heated arguments with a priest from the Yukon. He irritated and annoyed me no end. Again, only much later did I realize what annoyed me about this priest. His rigidity, his dogmatism and authoritarianism, his need to control, his own deep-seated insecurity were the very defects I was unwilling to face in myself.

In another of our private sessions, Marc used an image I have never forgotten. He suggested I was travelling through life inside an armoured tank and would only occasionally come up for air. The signals other people received from my swivelling guns were that I was a success, that I had it made, that I really didn't need anybody. The reality was that deep inside the tank was that same little child from Hastings huddled with fear and shivering with anxiety. I gave the impression I did not need the very thing I most craved - to be loved. I found the image of the tank informative, even illuminating. But ultimately, the image really didn't change anything, it didn't unravel the inner knot, it didn't silence, at least in any permanent way, the snarling dogs. Or to change the metaphor, to read an exciting and stimulating book on prayer doesn't mean you can pray.

What Southdown did was give me a respite, a breathing space, a feeling of refreshment and being cared for, a better sleep pattern than I had experienced in years. (As soon as I arrived, a doctor confiscated about 200 sleeping pills I had been saving as security.) Southdown also gave me for a time a feeling of solidity instead of shifting sand beneath my feet and introduced me to the solid values of a twelve-step program. The double rye and ginger I had had with Logie on our trip to Southdown would turn out to be my last drink.

So as the summer of 1969 turned into fall and the trees dotting the rolling hills turned to crimson and gold, a major decision began to form inside me. Gradually, but more insistently day by day, the decision became clear - I would leave the Jesuits. Why now? Why after a quarter of a century of uncertainty and vacillation? I think because, for the first time, the program and support I found at Southdown gave me the traction I needed to take a step I should have taken long before. I now had the physical rest, the clarity and the confidence to come to grips with my life as a Jesuit priest.

And what I saw in this new light - as though Southdown had changed the prescription for my glasses and I was seeing my life with a sharper clarity - what I now saw made no sense. I was not living any kind of spiritual life. I was habitually breaking my vow of chastity. It required more and more energy, and more and more booze, to maintain the outer façade to hide the inner turmoil. It caused too much stress to live as a performer or actor. (The Greek word for actor is *hypocrite*.) Except for the periods of congenial and successful external activity, I was not at peace with myself nor comfortable in my skin.

And there was something else, a reason that explains in part why I stayed in the Jesuit order for so long. For the first time, partially as a result of the hopefulness that Southdown instilled in me, I felt a surge of confidence I had never felt - I *would* be able to cope with the outside world. This new confidence well may have been the central motivating force in my decision to leave. That and a firm conviction that God would not punish me and that my friends and relatives, many of them Catholics, would accept me as an ex-Jesuit priest without considering me somehow disloyal and a failure. And so, without exception, they did.

113

12

THE SPECIAL OLYMPICS
AND A SPECIAL WEDDING

Early in November, 1969, I went to see the Jesuit provincial's assistant, Father Ed Dowling, to tell him of my decision to leave the Jesuits. He was understanding and supportive - as were the provincial himself, Father Robert Macdougall, and all my other Jesuit friends and associates. There was no hint of blame, no mention of the enormous sums of money the Jesuits had invested in my education and my health through a period of twenty-five years. Quite the contrary - I was invited to stay in my old room at Hawthorne Gardens until I could find a job.

So it was with optimism and enthusiasm that I began my job search in mid-November. Far from being stressed, once I had made the decision to leave the Jesuits, I experienced a feeling of peace, energy and well-being, in a word - liberation. This was perhaps the first mature decision I had ever made, mature in the sense that it was not dictated by the expectations of other people. So, looking for work, sometimes lining up as many as three or four appointments a day, was an adventure. Within six weeks of my forty-fifth birthday I was as excited as a teenager about what exciting prospects lay just around the corner.

I looked where I thought I had some strength - communications and publishing. An editorial position with a large publishing house fell through at the last minute as did another at TVOntario. I declined an entry-level reportorial job at *The Globe and Mail*. Then, at the suggestion of Father Gordie George, I went to see Harry E. "Red" Foster, the founder and owner of the successful advertising firm bearing his name.

Red Foster, then sixty-four, was a big man in body - he had been a star football player on the Balmy Beach Grey Cup champions - and a big man in spirit (a dynamic, ebullient mixture of business tycoon E.P. Taylor and Mother Teresa). In memory of his intellectually handicapped brother, Red Foster had established a foundation to advance the cause of the intellectually handicapped across Canada.

I went to see Foster, not about his advertising agency, but about his Foundation for the Intellectually Handicapped. I had heard that he could be as tough as nails, but I liked Red Foster right away and I think he liked me. After several searching interviews, he hired me as the first executive director of the Foster Foundation. It was the first real paying job I had ever had. I well remember the salary, $12,000 a year. Then for good measure, Red threw in the keys to his old family home at 4 Oaklands Avenue, just below De La Salle College, where I could live rent-free.

As I packed my trunk at Hawthorne Gardens in early March 1970, I could scarcely credit my good fortune, but it was tinged with a sadness for what was ending. In the trunk was the last official document I would ever receive from the Jesuit order. It was just three words relating to a decision already ratified in Rome about my dismissal from the Society of Jesus: *Litteras dismissionis accepit.* So few words to end so long a journey. Then Father Logie drove me the few short blocks to my new home at 4 Oaklands. We wrestled my trunk up to the second-floor living room. Logie left and I sat down and looked at the telephone, thinking to myself I could ring up the world. And I laughed out loud.

Working with Red Foster for the next two and a half years was like working for a threshing machine. There were speeches to write and sometimes deliver, meetings to attend and events to organize. But by far the most exciting element of the job was Red's association with the Kennedy Foundation in the States. The Foundation was headed by the late President's sister Eunice and her husband, Sargent Shriver. As a result of this connection, we introduced the Special Olympics for the Intellectually Handicapped into Canada and convinced the Kennedys to accept floor hockey as part of the Special Olympics program. Red persuaded the National Hockey League to support floor hockey and we convinced Prime Minister Trudeau to throw out the puck at the first floor hockey tournament, which was held at Maple Leaf Gardens in Toronto.

I represented Red at the first Special Olympics ever held in Quebec, on St. Helen's Island in Montreal. Then we flew to Washington to attend two events hosted by the Kennedy Foundation. The first was a seminar on the rights of the intellectually handicapped, attended by Senator Edward Kennedy and Mother Teresa. The second was the presentation of a Kennedy award to Jean Vanier, son of the former Governor General and founder of l'Arche community homes for the intellectually handicapped. Some time later we flew with a television crew to West Palm Beach to interview Rose Kennedy. The footage was used as part of our campaign to raise money for the Special Olympics in Canada.

But the highlight of my time with Red Foster did not involve big-name people. It involved the intellectually handicapped themselves. One event stands out - the first Canadian National Special Olympics, which were held at the CNE and Ontario Place in June 1971. Enormous preparation had gone into organizing these games and teams had been entered from all ten provinces. On a warm June evening, the opening ceremonies took place on the track in front of the grandstand at the CNE grounds. There they all were - the dignitaries, the Lieutenant Governor in his gold braid, Premier William Davis and his wife, city officials, aides in their glittering uniforms, the military, bands and cheerleaders.

Then I looked down the track. A band came into view, its martial music reverberating through the grandstand. Next, from each of the ten provinces came bearers with their banners and flags gently flapping in the warm breeze. And behind the banners came the special athletes, the Olympians, carrying in their hearts their special oath: "Let me win. But if I cannot win, let me be brave in the attempt." Some of them stumbled a bit, others walked haltingly, still others tried to do a little jig, but all of them - representing their country from coast to coast - beamed and waved and smiled at the rest of us in a kind of happy blessing. I smiled back at them, these special people. I looked at their faces warm in the setting sun and watched them dancing to the music - and suddenly I choked up. I, also handicapped, in my own halting way was trying to reach out to them, to respond to their courage and their love. And I started to cry.

During this exciting period working for Red Foster, I had plenty of time to socialize and make new friends, such as Bill Belyea who helped me navigate the workaday world. Denise and I saw less and less of each other as I tried to put old patterns behind me. My counsellor at Southdown, Mark Eveson, warned me to make no major decision for at least a year. But that left plenty of room for action. I took up ballroom dancing, joining a group called Hiatus which billed itself as an Arts and

Letters Society with a sense of humour. And I met several women with whom I had brief relationships but no commitments.

Not until the beginning of 1972, that is. I was hosting a social evening for Hiatus at my house. The speaker was Professor Ramsay Cook, probably English-Canada's leading expert on Quebec nationalism. In the course of the evening I met another member of Hiatus. She was tall and slim, had blond hair and striking blue eyes, and her name was Catharine Fleming Turnbull. Some time later we met again on the dance floor at another Hiatus party. I was intrigued and asked her out for dinner and more dancing. I sensed that somehow Catharine was different from other women. We had a long, inconclusive discussion about appropriate sexual behaviour and that is where we left it.

Six months later the phone rang in my office. It was Catharine calling from her office. She was a speech writer with the Ontario Ministry of Education at Queen's Park. Had I seen the reference to my Hepburn book in *The Globe and Mail*? Indeed I had, which was not important. What was important was that the phone call unleashed an emotional avalanche that moved with blinding speed and quickly engulfed us both.

I arranged to see Catharine that same evening in early May 1972. For the next ten nights straight we went out dining, dancing or to the theatre. Sometimes Catharine would come for breakfast. I also began sending flowers and telegrams to her office on a daily basis. This was about as normal for me as getting up at midnight to floss my teeth. But nothing was normal these days. I was in a new space, one I had never inhabited before. This wasn't puppy love in Hyde Park or infatuation over a weekend. This was the real thing. I had sensed in Catharine a depth both mysterious and translucent, a spiritual quality that rang true. Add to that an effervescent sense of humour and a musical laugh that tinkled like Christmas bells. Would she marry me? Yes, she would. I don't understand now why we waited ten days.

That same evening, Catharine went to a large family gathering where she told her mother she had become engaged. A few days later I was invited to meet her mother, Victoria, in her elegantly furnished apartment off Avenue Road below St. Clair. In some respects Victoria, affectionately called "Aunt Queenie" by her close friends and family, fitted the description of a *mulier fortis*, a matriarch, in the Old Testament. She was a woman of character, faith and wisdom garnered over long years rich in experience, people and giving to others. Her life was centred on her extended family. Her father, Robert J. Fleming, "the people's Bob," had been mayor of Toronto in the 1890s. Her husband, Walter Turnbull, a Protestant missionary, had been killed in a car accident before their only daughter, Catharine, was born. Victoria never remarried but devoted her life to her family, her friends and her many charities, especially those related to the church.

So in terms of backgrounds our meeting was a curious one. Victoria had come from a long line of northern Irish forebears rooted in the Protestant tradition, a tradition that viewed Irish Catholics and some of their superstitions and drinking habits with, not to put too fine a point on it, some suspicion. And here I was in her spacious living room, not only an Irish Catholic but a former Jesuit priest, ostensibly asking for the hand of her only daughter in marriage - "ostensibly," as the question was academic, since Catharine, like her mother, had a strong mind of her own and had already made it up. Nevertheless, Victoria expressed her concerns about our relationship, then explained to me how she and her large family had been praying since Catharine was a little girl that the Lord would provide the right husband for her. Summoning all the years of Jesuit training going back to Aristotle's advice on how to make one's case, I replied quickly, "All your prayers have now been answered." In spite of herself, Aunt Queenie's sense of humour surfaced and we both relaxed into our chairs and began to discuss plans for the wedding.

There was one problem that seemed insuperable. It was one thing for Victoria to agree to her daughter's marrying a Catholic; it was quite another to agree the marriage should take place in a Catholic church with a Catholic priest. Catharine told me frankly this would be asking too much of her mother. So we took our problem to a senior official in the Catholic Archdiocese who promised to take it higher. To my relief, Archbishop Pocock gave permission to have a Protestant minister officiate at our marriage.

So on August 19, 1972, a hot cloudless day, Catharine and I were married in the chapel at Bishop Strachan School which she had attended. An old friend of Catharine's family, Canon Dann of the Anglican Cathedral, presided at the ceremony, assisted by my good Jesuit friend, Father Edward Dowling. Afterwards the reception for our families and friends was held at the Hunt Club overlooking the sparkling waters of Lake Ontario. We drove to Muskoka for a few days of canoeing and swimming, then to the shores of Lake Simcoe to Victoria's splendid sixty-year-old summer home, Peribonka, named for the river in Quebec where she and Walter had spent their honeymoon. For Catharine and me on our honeymoon on Lake Simcoe, they were happy days.

13

BROADCASTING AND BENEDICTINES

After our honeymoon, it was back to business in Toronto. Perhaps it would be a new business since I had little more to contribute to the Foster Foundation. So I answered an advertisement in *The Globe and Mail* for a director of public affairs at a large metropolitan radio station, which turned out to be CJAD in Montreal. CJAD had the reputation of being one of the best stations in the country. After an audition and several trips to Montreal for intensive interviews, I was hired over fifty-six other candidates. So Catharine and I said our good-byes and packed our bags. Finally we were ready to leave Toronto. I remember the moment exactly. We and the movers packing our furniture had been listening to the last game of the Canada-Russia hockey series. Suddenly Paul Henderson scored the winning Canadian goal over the Russians in Moscow. Everyone was yelling and cheering as we went out the door.

So, on the morning of October 4, 1972, at the age of forty-seven, I walked into the studios of CJAD and joined a staff managed by the legendary Mac McCurdy. On the staff was George Balcan, considered by many the best morning man in Canadian radio. I could scarcely believe my good fortune. Editorials, interviews, round tables - I developed a taste for them all, but I never really hit my stride at CJAD until the station manager, Ted Blackman, suggested I co-host a live talk show to be called *Exchange* with Hélène Gougeon, an excellent broadcaster. Later, I would host it by myself.

And so, assisted by Trish McKenna, my enthusiastic producer, I began almost ten years of the most exciting radio job imaginable, being plugged in daily for two hours in mid-morning to a wide segment of Montrealers. We discussed everything from abortion to how you get on with your mate while driving your car, which turned out to be one of the zaniest programs we ever did. Live talk radio is both intimate and anonymous, simple yet enormously flexible. We did programs on incest where callers spoke for the first time in their lives about their dreadful experiences. We talked with an eyewitness to the Sadat assassination shortly after it happened, with legislators in Quebec City after the soldier started shooting in the National Assembly, and once when we were discussing a women's orchestra in a Nazi concentration camp, a man called in who had been in the camp and had attended their concerts.

Just before Christmas one year, two children called to say they were collecting food for the poor and asked others to help them. For two hours, listeners called from east and west Montreal, offering to set up food depots, provide transport and collect nonperishables. Before the end of the day, the initial loaves and fishes had been multiplied enough to feed nearly 4,000 Montrealers. During the 1980 referendum, we made it not only possible but comfortable for federalists and separatists to talk with each other on *Exchange*.

In all the years I was hosting *Exchange*, there is no question which program provoked the most uproar. It involved Brian Mulroney when he was still Conservative opposition leader. He agreed to be a guest on the program but his staff stipulated he would not take any calls. Going onto a call-in show and refusing to take calls made about as much sense as going into a TV studio and refusing to turn on the lights. Our listeners couldn't understand it. *The Toronto Star* got wind of it and on the morning of the show put the story on its front page. By the time he arrived at CJAD, which was packed with TV and radio people from other stations, Mr. Mulroney had heard about the criticism and was in a rage. With just minutes to air, my able producer, Holly Haimerl, told me I was being summoned to the station manager's office. There, Mr. Mulroney, perspiring and red-faced, proceeded to excoriate me for causing him political embarrassment - although we had warned his staff they should not try to insulate him. "Why," he said, "should I waste my time talking to English Montrealers? They are all Liberals anyway." But Brian Mulroney was nothing if not an astute politician. At some point amidst all the media hubbub, he sensed that he had more to lose politically by ducking the program than by going ahead and facing the music, or in this case, the questions. So he stood up, squared his shoulders, adopted a thin smile and went on the air. Ultimately, he handled about a dozen calls, almost all of them favourable to him. I did not see him again until he was Prime Minister. We had a short, friendly chat at a St. Patrick's Ball, then I heard him say to an aide, "I think McKenty has mellowed."

Those were the days when CJAD had a generous travel budget. Once I was sent to Washington to sit in on the Watergate hearings that led to the impeachment of President Nixon. I chatted with Nixon's chief aide, John Ehrlichman (who later went to prison), about whether a Watergate crime could happen in Canada. Another time I managed to get myself into a press conference with Ronald Reagan. It was like winning the lottery when President Reagan picked me to ask a question - which, somewhat to my delight, clearly annoyed him.

The most rewarding episode of my radio career involved a taxi driver who had won a City of Montreal medal for bravery. He had jumped into the cab of an empty truck whose brakes had failed and which was rolling toward a schoolyard filled with children. He somehow managed to wrestle the truck to a stop. Unfortunately, he wrenched his back in the incident and couldn't work, and his wife also was an invalid. He had the medal but no money. I told his story on CJAD, opened up the lines on the popular *Paul Reid Show*, and within two hours we had collected $13,000 - a dramatic example of the power of radio and the generosity of Montrealers.

Beneath the outward success and excitement of my radio work, however, there began to re-emerge an inner anxiety and agitation. It displayed itself in bursts of anger at home with Catharine and at work with my colleagues, as though just beneath my placid exterior there was a pool of rage like glowing lava waiting to erupt. At the station I felt most comfortable and most energized when actually doing the talk show. It seemed to provide a structure in which I was totally in control. I often found it more stressful to relate to my colleagues in person than to talk with listeners on air. About this time I began to see, on an informal basis, a psychiatrist at the Montreal General Hospital. My main complaints related to my insomnia and the feeling that I had no friends at the station. Of course I had friends at the station. But what counted was my perception, not the reality. More and more I was retreating inside my armoured tank, desperately trying to give the impression that I didn't care, that I had everything under control. l was becoming increasingly uncomfortable in my skin.

About this same time, despite a happy marriage and challenging jobs, Catharine and I felt there was something missing in our lives, a spiritual dimension of some kind. We began to search for a guide and, thanks to a word from a former Jesuit colleague, we discovered Dom John Main, a Benedictine monk who had come to Montreal in 1977 to start a meditation centre in a dilapidated house in Notre Dame de Grâce. John Main, then about fifty, was a tall, impressive looking man with a military bearing, a ready wit - redolent of his beloved County Kerry, his family's early home - and a voice modulated like an actor's, which indeed, in another dispensation, he might have been.

John Main had been taught by the Jesuits. He had joined a British intelligence unit during the war, studied and taught law at Trinity College in Dublin, and spent a couple of years in Malaya in the mid-1950s with the British Civil Service. It was in Malaya that John Main's interest in prayer was further developed by a Hindu swami who taught him silent meditation using a sacred word, or mantra. Much to his delight, after he became a Benedictine monk at Ealing in London - where the famous Trappist monk, Thomas Merton had been born - John Main discovered this form of silent meditation using a mantra was also deeply imbedded in the Christian tradition.

So it was to teach Christian meditation that John Main, accompanied by a young Benedictine associate, Laurence Freeman, came to Montreal at the invitation of Bishop Leonard Crowley. Catharine and I began going weekly to his talks and we started to meditate twice a day. One of the fruits of meditation that Catharine noticed was that my bursts of anger became less frequent and I was more relaxed and easier to live with. We continued our attendance after John Main moved his meditation centre to Pine Avenue, on the slopes of Mount Royal, into a large mansion, a magnificent gift of the McConnell Foundation. McConnell had been publisher of *The Montreal Star*. I remember spending one weekend there and generously offering to clean the carpets outside John Main's room. Unfortunately, my cleaning was tying the carpets into knots. It was only when John Main himself came out to see what the trouble was that I discovered I was not using a carpet cleaner but a floor polisher.

Sadly, John Main was not able to develop the community he had hoped for at the Benedictine Priory on Pine Avenue. Cancer, which had been successfully treated in 1979, recurred, and he died at the early age of fifty-six on December 30, 1982. To my surprise, Dom Laurence Freeman O.S.B., John Main's associate and his successor as Prior of the Benedictine community, asked me on the night of Father John's death if I would be interested in writing John Main's biography. I immediately agreed, and over the next three years our research took Catharine and me to Ireland and England. We also went to Washington, where John

124

Main had been headmaster of a private boys' school in the early seventies. The biography, *In the Stillness Dancing*, was published in London and New York in 1986 and again by Unitas Books in Montreal in 1995. It was well reviewed, and I have always been grateful to Father Laurence Freeman for giving me the opportunity to do it.

While I was researching and writing the biography, I decided to give notice to CJAD that I would have to leave. The decision had nothing to do with the success of my talk show, *Exchange*, and the immense pleasure I derived from doing it. In fact, my old friend Ted Blackman tried to persuade me to move to his new station, CFCF. When I remained at CJAD, Blackman, always a fighter, decided to give me a run for my money. He hired a strong talk-show team - the well-known Liberal Solange Chaput-Rolland, the heavyweight separatist, Pierre Bourgault and the journalist and future Mulroney biographer, L. Ian MacDonald. They never really got off the ground, and when I left CJAD in July 1985, the ratings for *Exchange* were at their highest ever and the lines were still blazing. My only reason for leaving was because I felt I could not do justice to both the radio program and the John Main biography. Now, years later, I still believe that if one is doing radio, hosting a live talk show is the thing to do, and for me, at any rate, CJAD was the best place to do it.

After returning from Ireland in the summer of 1987, where the John Main biography had been launched at Trinity College, I was astonished to receive a telephone call from a senior program producer at CFCF Television, Don McGowan, a well-known Montreal television personality in his own right. Over lunch at the garden café of the Ritz-Carlton, McGowan asked me if I would be interested in doing a live talk show on television, a sort of poor man's *Larry King Live*. McGowan would provide a chauffeur-driven limousine to pick me up each morning (impressive for the neighbours) and an extensive new wardrobe (a delight for Catharine who never approved of my doing radio in a scruffy T-shirt).

Of course I jumped at the opportunity, and in September 1987, we went on the air with Montreal's first English live call-in television program, *McKenty Live*. Television is more cumbersome and complicated than radio, but for the next three years I had a lot of fun - the limousine with a bar, telephone and TV set in the back seat; the warmth and soft hands in the make-up room; a small, friendly staff. During the three years we had some remarkable guests: the famous sexologist, Dr. Ruth, who was so tiny she had to sit on a Montreal telephone directory; Canada's chief negotiator, Louis Reisman, with whom I had a ferocious argument on free trade two days before the federal election; and René Lévesque, the only guest who not only smoked, but offered a cigarette to everyone in the crew. Only a week later, this man whom I liked very much, died of a heart attack. René Lévesque's last appearance in public might well have been on *McKenty Live*.

When people ask me who was the most interesting person I ever interviewed, the answer is always Gilles Thibault. When he was about twelve, he was a boarder in a school run by the Christian brothers near Rigaud, Quebec. One morning Gilles learned that his mother, a prostitute - who was paying for his education - had died in Montreal. He was refused permission to go to her funeral, so he stole a bicycle and went anyway. He was apprehended for stealing the bicycle and sent to a detention centre. In 1945 he was sent to Bordeaux Prison for robbery, where he was assigned to a detail which cut down hanged prisoners. Until he was finally released from the maximum security Archambault Prison in 1988, Gilles Thibault had spent a total of forty-two years in prison, mainly for armed robbery. As he told me, he wasn't very good at it. He spent much time in isolation and often received the lash. One night, thinking about suicide, he knelt down beside the bed in his cell and asked God, if there was a God, to help him. At that point Gilles Thibault seems to have had a genuine spiritual experience which changed his life.

After reading his memoir, *J'ai passé 42 ans en prison*, I expected to meet an angry and bitter person, resentful that he had been short-changed by life. Not at all. He was now nearly sixty, a trim, smiling, fit man, neatly dressed, articulate in two languages. He knew who he was, who he had been, and he knew the difference. There was no self-pity. He regretted what he had done. Now he was getting on with his life. He was a whole person. In a quiet, confident voice he answered calls, many of them from ex-cons or prisoners on parole. I was especially pleased when a senior officer of the MUC police called to congratulate Gilles on what he had made of his life. Over the years in radio and television, I had many movers and shakers as guests, but the one most memorable is Gilles Thibault.

Although I enjoyed *McKenty Live* and my associates on the program, Daniel Freedman, Wendy Helfenbaum and Bernie Peissel, at

126

the end of the third season, I decided to leave the program. My reasoning was: I would be repeating programs we had already done; some of my associates were being changed; I wanted to do some more writing, perhaps a book on Catharine's grandfather, onetime mayor of Toronto; and both Catharine and I were busy with the Benedictine Priory and meditation. So in June 1990, I left CFCF Television.

Since Dom John Main's death at the end of 1982, Catharine and I had become more involved in the Priory on Pine Avenue. We had helped start a world-wide newsletter, *Unitas*, and had given workshops on Christian meditation both in Canada and the United States. Catharine was the coordinator for several international meditation conferences in Montreal and I had assisted her by moderating the plenary group discussions. We both participated in a school of prayer in Dublin and another international conference at York in England. One event I remember at the Priory was a luncheon attended by Yehudi Menuhin and Pierre Trudeau, both meditators at that time. Through all these activities, Catharine and I made many friends both in Canada and abroad and we felt at the centre of the work Dom John Main had begun. The Priory had become a strong reference point for both of us.

After John Main's death in 1982, he was succeeded as Prior by his close associate, Dom Laurence Freeman. At that time Father Freeman was just over thirty - a bright, engaging, articulate young man who had a degree from Oxford University and who had worked with the United Nations. Still, despite Father Laurence's accomplishments, succeeding John Main at so early an age was a daunting challenge. But he pitched in with energy and enthusiasm. He tried to carry on the traditional roles of the Priory: a place where people came to learn Christian meditation, a retreat where people could stay for periods of time, and also a house where still others could follow a program to see whether they had a Benedictine vocation. He also tried to build up the Benedictine community on Pine Avenue, where much of the activity revolved around manual work, studies and daily periods of meditation, and he established a women's group across the street - Benedicta House - led by Benedictine Sisters from Minnesota. Much of their work involved hospitality. Father Laurence travelled extensively to teach Christian meditation throughout the world and gathered around himself a group of devoted friends. Under his leadership, the Priory seemed to be thriving. But underneath, problems were simmering, and they boiled over with dramatic suddenness.

Perhaps one warning signal should have been the high turnover of young men who came to the Priory as a testing-ground. Why did they not stay? It was also significant that none of Father Laurence's Benedictine colleagues came to Montreal to assist him in the work of meditation. The monastic community at the Priory was not developing in any consistent or healthy way. So it was almost inevitable that tension would emerge between those who wanted to build a stable community - stability was a cornerstone of St. Benedict's monastic vision - and those who wanted to devote their energies to expanding the work of Christian meditation.

Eventually these tensions, exacerbated by personality conflicts endemic to any religious community, became so painful that a team of conflict-resolution professionals was brought in from the United States to evaluate the situation, deflate the tensions and help the community work through its problems. Then, during a meeting with one of the conciliation experts present, there was a blow-up between Father Laurence and members of the women's community which resulted in the destruction of the community. As a result, about half the Benedictine community left, including the superior of the women's group, Sister Christian Morris, OSB, an able and dedicated nun. Paul Geraghty also left. He was a talented monk who had been a barrister in England and the only priest, other than Father Laurence himself, who had been associated with Dom John Main from the beginning. This was a bewildering period for most meditators, including myself. It only emerged much later that the basic problem leading to the breakup of the Priory was a loss of trust in the way decisions were being made by Father Laurence.

For some months the Priory continued to function but it never fully recovered from the overthrow of the women's community in May 1989. A little more than a year later Father Laurence resigned as Prior and withdrew to London, England. He was succeeded in September 1990 by an engaging monk, William Main, Father John's nephew who had managed the Main hotel in Ballinskelligs, County Kerry.

At the beginning of 1991 came another bombshell. Without a warning it was announced that the Priory would be closed at least temporarily and the teaching of Christian meditation would be suspended indefinitely. The reason given (only some time later) was lack of numbers - only two Benedictine monks still lived at the Priory. The Montreal Christian meditation community was stunned by this news which we could not comprehend. Up to this point I had been a strong supporter of Laurence Freeman's leadership. More than that, we had become friends, partly because of his generous help on the John Main biography. I had concluded that the collapse of the women's community had been due to a personality conflict and now the closing of the Priory I put down to faulty judgement. About this time, Father Laurence telephoned me from England and asked me to minimize as much as I could the news of the Priory's closing.

Shortly after the call from Father Laurence, I received another call, this time from Father Laurence's immediate Benedictine superiors, asking me to come to a series of meetings at the Priory. I considered the matter under discussion, primarily Father Laurence's leadership, so serious that I took notes at these meetings. The concerns expressed by Father Laurence's superiors on his leadership were concentrated in three areas: his exercise of control, his questionable relationships, and his frequent absences. On the control issue, it was felt that Father Laurence, despite an appearance of delegating authority, ultimately kept control in his own hands and exercised it through surrogates even when he was absent. In connection with the issue of control, the question arose as to whom Father Laurence was accountable. As a practical matter, there did not seem to be any satisfactory answer.

On the matter of personal relationships, concern was expressed that Father Laurence showed favouritism and had special friendships often outside the Benedictines which were destructive to community building. Finally, his frequent and sometimes lengthy absences from the Priory, on the quite legitimate work of teaching meditation, too often left the monastic community with a lack of direction and support. Eleven young men had come and gone in one fourteen-month period, another example of lack of stability. Even the two monks who remained, Leonard Montone and William Main, made it clear that they no longer wished to be associated with Father Laurence. As a result of these perceived defects in his leadership and his failure to build any viable monastic community, Father Laurence's superiors decided the Priory should be closed and turned over to the Roman Catholic Archdiocese of Montreal. In subsequent discussions, I learned that officials in the Archdiocese were equally concerned about Father Laurence's leadership.

These meetings with Father Laurence's Benedictine superiors on his leadership perplexed me. The picture I had of a community with normal growing pains was shattered. One of the strongest reference points I had, the Priory, was being called into question. Of course I had heard vague criticism of Father Laurence's leadership before but never gave it any credence. In fact, I had lost friends because I supported Father Laurence right down the line. Now, as I listened to his superiors and to others who had lived under him as Prior, I became increasingly concerned. Questions I had never addressed before now had to be addressed. But because of our friendship and long collaboration, I thought it only fair that I should raise these leadership problems with him directly. This was all the more urgent because discussions were going forward about establishing a lay community at the Priory after the last monks left. When he had visited Montreal early in 1991, Father Laurence had given me a memorandum in which he suggested possible directors and members for the new lay community.

So after he returned to Montreal in March from a trip to the United States, I arranged to have lunch with him at the home of a mutual friend. During a two-hour conversation before lunch I raised with Father Laurence the concerns his superiors had discussed with me. His response was that the concerns were unfounded and that a former associate was trying to blacken his reputation. I then introduced the possibility of a meeting in Montreal involving Father Laurence and his superiors with representation from the meditation community to air all the concerns about his leadership. He declined this proposal and future discussions did not resolve the issues that had been raised.

At the end of what proved to be my last conversation with Father Laurence, I felt a keen sadness. I watched him walking down the front steps after lunch, pulling up the collar of his thin and somewhat threadbare winter coat against the snow and cold. Then the door was closed behind him and I sensed a door had also closed on our friendship. But I also experienced a sense of loss, even of betrayal, that our journey together, Laurence's and mine, had ended in ashes: the priory closing, the women's community destroyed, and the work of John Main damaged.

Regretfully, I concluded I could no longer be associated with Laurence Freeman's leadership in Montreal. As a practical matter, this decision was not complicated because his superiors had decided to restrict his ministry in this city. He had been recalled to his home monastery in New York State where four possible choices for the future were discussed with him. None of these involved returning to Montreal to teach meditation at the Priory. All these decisions made by Father Laurence's superiors were concurred with by officials of the Archdiocese of Montreal who expressed the view that the Christian meditation community in Montreal should "turn the page on Father Laurence."

These painful developments had the immediate effect of dividing what had been a fairly close-knit meditation group. Some who felt Father Laurence had been treated unjustly made their views known to his superiors and to other church authorities. They expressed their concern that some members of the Benedictine community itself and several meditators were trying to ruin Laurence's reputation for their own ends (although these ends were never revealed); they attributed the breakup of the Priory to the disobedience of the Benedictine community living under Laurence and to the refusal of other Benedictines to come to Montreal to help him, and to the weak leadership of William Main; they were suspicious that money collected for the work of Christian meditation (much of it through the efforts of the Archdiocese) would be diverted to other purposes; and they feared losing their teacher who was irreplaceable.

There is no doubt in my mind that these views were held sincerely and in good faith. There was also no doubt that, on the basis of my conversations with Laurence Freeman's superiors, I could not, in good conscience, subscribe to these views. These were sad and destructive days for the Benedictine Priory and for the vision John Main and Father Laurence himself had brought so generously to Montreal more than a dozen years earlier. No one was more upset than Bishop Leonard Crowley, who had so many high hopes for the enterprise of silent prayer at a time when there was so much turmoil in Quebec.

The result of these sad events was that the Benedictine Priory closed as a priory when the last monk and the last Prior, William Main, left in May 1991. Nevertheless, Christian meditation groups continued to meet and Christian meditation continued to be taught at the centre John Main had founded on Pine Avenue, under a lay committee to which I was appointed chairman by Archbishop Jean-Claude Turcotte. Laurence Freeman returned to London where he eventually joined a small Benedictine community. He and his associates launched the World Community of Christian Meditation to promote the teaching of meditation, which it has done with considerable success. Those Montreal meditators who felt Laurence Freeman was treated unjustly continue to follow him as their teacher. Those other Montreal meditators who had concerns about his leadership still meet at the centre John Main founded, now called Unitas, but they have not joined the international meditation organization, nor has Dom John Main's sister Yvonne, who promotes her brother's work in Ireland.

It was about this time that I received sad news from Hastings. My brother, Stafford, had died. He had retired after thirty years of productive service in the hardware business in Kingston. After raising their three splendid children, he and Sue had returned to Hastings and built a home there. Then his health problems caught up with him and he died from complications from a stroke at the age of sixty-three. My brother was a gentle person. I can't think of anyone he ever deliberately hurt. Looking back now, I wish we had both known how to connect more often before "too soon it was too late."

After the collapse of the Priory, I turned to another problem, my chronic insomnia. Perhaps the turmoil over Laurence Freeman's leadership and over Stafford's death exacerbated the problem. In any event, in April 1991, I was so tired of being in a funk over lack of sleep that I determined to make a major effort to lick it. So I drove to Toronto and signed myself into the Donwood Clinic for addiction treatment and remained there a month. It was a good month, similar to my time at Southdown, with a relaxed atmosphere, group therapy and recreation, and Catharine's visits on weekends. I managed to get off sleeping pills entirely and took the train back to Montreal relaxed and refreshed.

When the warm weather came, I took up golf with more zest and began to enjoy it. Then one afternoon when I returned from my golf game there was a telephone message from our family doctor, Mark Roper. As a result of my last regular checkup he had discovered a spot on my lung. He arranged for me to see the Surgeon-in-Chief at the Montreal General Hospital, David Mulder, who told me he wanted it understood that he would level with me all the way, no beating around the bush. That was the way I wanted it and it wasn't long before I discovered I was in the hands of one of the best surgeons on the continent. Dr. Mulder told me there was a "jagged, angry-looking shadow" on the lung and there was roughly a seventy percent chance it was cancerous.

I felt what was to be, was to be, and continued to play golf every day while I waited for a bed at the General. Finally in July, Dr. Mulder, in what is considered a difficult procedure, operated by separating some ribs and removing a large growth which turned out to be benign. I was home in ten days, and in three weeks was playing golf again - very gingerly.

Early in the fall, Catharine began to coordinate the first all-Canadian Christian meditation conference, to be held in November. Long before the demise of the Priory, Father Laurence had agreed that he would give the keynote address. On the afternoon of the day the conference was to begin, intense pressure was brought to bear from several quarters, including a bishop in Ontario, that a meeting be convened immediately to heal the growing split in the Montreal meditation community between those who acknowledged Laurence Freeman's leadership and those who did not. There was a lot of talk about reconciliation between the two groups but no talk of acknowledging responsibility for what had happened - an altogether unsatisfactory approach akin to picking at a scab while ignoring the infection. It seemed to me and others I consulted that such a meeting at that time would merely transfer the sham that had existed at the Priory to a second sham that would envelop the entire meditation community.

As might be expected there was considerable tension as the conference began in a spacious convent on the West Island. Personally, I found the atmosphere extremely upsetting, not to say hostile. People who had meditated together for years and become friends were scarcely speaking to each other. At the plenary session I rose and angrily accused those I felt had helped destroy the Priory of now trying to destroy the group that continued to meet in the centre begun by John Main which Father Laurence's group had by then abandoned. In retrospect, there is no question my intervention was not a helpful one and even if it had to be said, as a dear friend and fellow-meditator wrote me later, she wished I had said it out of love rather than anger. Laurence Freeman himself replied to my angry outburst with a denial and a defense of his own leadership. At that point the tension and antagonism became so palpable that the capable and experienced moderator asked for fifteen minutes of silent meditation to allow the animosity to simmer down.

For a long time I was puzzled and upset by the depth of my anger against Laurence Freeman and some of his supporters at the meditation conference. Now looking back on what happened I believe there is an explanation. Part of this is that I saw in Laurence Freeman a defect that I refused to face in myself - the need to control others, a need that often disguises an inner fear and anxiety that must be kept hidden at all costs. Laurence gave the impression of delegating authority, gave articulate lip service to collective leadership, but on closer examination this was only an impression. Even when he put someone else in charge, he continued to pull the strings - which was one reason the only remaining Benedictines had decided to leave.

This kind of control, as I know from my own experience, cannot abide an outside challenge or tolerate dissent because this might reveal the inner fears and anxieties that the mask of rigid control is trying to disguise. I believe this refusal to tolerate an opposing view resulted in the destruction of the women's community. When Laurence Freeman's superiors were evaluating his leadership style, what concerned them most was the abuse of spiritual power and the resulting damage to others. To remain in a state of denial about this was all the easier for Father Laurence because of the degree of autonomy he enjoyed at the Priory.

Another source of my intemperate expression of anger against Father Laurence was the split, with which I had been familiar all my life, between what was preached on the outside and what really existed on the inside. I had experienced this split, this double-dealing, with my father, with some priests in my childhood, with certain aspects of my Jesuit formation, in the way I myself dealt with other people - and then suddenly the same malaise emerged again at the Priory under Laurence Freeman. There was this split between appearances and reality which had done so much damage in my own life and which could only be put to rights by an admission of responsibility, a giving up of control, leading to the process of healing.

I wish I had not responded to Father Laurence's need for control with so much anger of my own. These feelings of anger and indeed fear became even more scary when both Catharine and I realized we were being made scapegoats for the divisions in the Montreal meditation community. After years at the heart of the work in Montreal, we gradually found ourselves marginalized and isolated. The last night of the conference I told Catharine I had taken eight sleeping pills and was thinking of suicide. The dogs were snarling again - a portent of darker days to come.

14

CLINICAL DEPRESSION

After the stress of the meditation conference, Catharine and I drove to Florida to stay a month in the lovely holiday home of our Montreal friends John and Clare Hallward. This vacation took our minds off the sad difficulties with some of our other friends in Montreal. I played golf, badly, almost every day. We also visited two of the wisest and most spiritual people we know, both in their nineties, Jim and Ellie Newton. They had devoted the years after the war to working for permanent peace and reconciliation, much of this recounted in Jim's book, *Uncommon Friends*. Uncommon indeed. Jim knew Thomas Edison well and Henry Ford, had worked for Harvey Firestone, fraternized with the Nobel prize winner, Dr. Alexis Carrel, and explored the Everglades with his close friend, Charles Lindbergh. A visit with Jim and Ellie Newton always raised our spirits.

The separation problem in Quebec was becoming more serious. In the new year, refreshed from our Florida sojourn, I joined with John Hallward and a small group to organize an advertising campaign and media interviews in a number of cities across Canada in the cause of national unity. After the excitement of this campaign, there was a bit of a letdown. At first it was nothing more than a funk that took some of the sunshine from my day. Nothing more, that is, until July 1992. Then the ferocious fury of the snarling dogs, leashed for so many years by religion, success, sex, friends and alcohol, engulfed me.

As those who write about clinical depression admit, we have no language to describe it adequately. In my opinion, the American novelist William Styron has done it best in *Darkness Visible*. To compare depression to prolonged and acute "blues," a malaise we all experience from time to time, would be like comparing an April shower to a tornado. They are of a different magnitude entirely. As the fall of 1992 deepened into winter, I felt the emotional turbulence of all the past years - the anger, the anxiety, the fear, the loneliness, the shame, the resentment - like a clogged toilet backing up and overflowing into my bloodstream and my brain with all the stinking and poisonous detritus of a lifetime's dis-ease. I say the brain, and no doubt depression is a malady of the brain. But depression, as felt and experienced, is a sickness of the spirit, a cancer metastasizing from the soul.

The emotional poison circulating through my system undoubtedly affected my body, rendering it sluggish, lethargic, at times virtually paralyzed. But it devastated my spirit. My soul became mouldy like mildew on stale bread; my outlook on life was grey and desolate. This desolation was usually worse in the morning. I found it difficult, sometimes impossible, to get out of bed. What was the point? I had nothing I wanted to do. Certainly there was no one I wished to see. At the urging of Catharine, I summoned the energy to go to the psychiatric clinic at the Montreal General Hospital where I was referred to Dr. Pablo Cervantes, the Director of the Mood Disorders Clinic.

And so began almost two years of a horror I never could have dreamed existed. I can only describe it as plunging into a black hole with no hope of rescue. For me these were the two salient characteristics of clinical depression - darkness and hopelessness. But these general horrors had their own particular sub-species - despondency and gloom. I felt my life had been a waste and a failure. As I looked back over the years in Hastings, in the Jesuits and in the media, there was no sliver of satisfaction, only the overwhelming sensation of unreality and hypocrisy. I felt a knot of self-hatred and loathing. If ever I had had any friends, they were gone now. I was utterly alone. This was the grown version of the frightened little boy in Hastings in the bell jar, who couldn't connect with anybody, who never felt he fitted in.

I had never fitted, never connected, so now I withdrew from further efforts to maintain the façade. I stayed for most of the day on the couch in the living room with the blinds down and the curtains drawn. I lost my appetite for food, any desire for sex and any interest in people. When the telephone rang I did not answer. When in the morning after a cup of coffee and a piece of dry toast, I drew down the blinds, retreated to the couch and pulled the covers over my head, I felt a modicum of relief. No decisions, no appointments, no need to smile, to please, or keep up a front. For a few hours I was safe in my cocoon.

There was one regular break in this oppressive and deadly routine. Thanks to an assignment from my good friend, Gord Sinclair, news director at my old station, CJAD, I went into the station every weekday afternoon to participate in a live-discussion panel on current affairs called *Free-for-All*. Some days it was excruciatingly difficult to move - the couch acted like a magnet holding me in the safety of its field until I made a Herculean effort to escape its influence. Because she thought the physical exercise would help, Catharine urged me to walk to CJAD. But I usually drove the car and returned to the security of the couch as soon as the program was over.

As my desolate mood merged with the greyness of winter, Catharine and I talked about taking some kind of break, perhaps a cruise. But whenever we discussed a cruise, I raised the possibility of committing suicide by jumping off the ship. As winter deepened I talked more and more about suicide. Life was not worth living. There was no place for me, no way out of the dark tunnel, no possibility of ever again leashing the snarling dogs. So the thought of suicide became more attractive as the only way out, and the thought kept running around in my head like a record that had become stuck and I didn't know how to turn it off.

In February 1993, with Catharine's cousin Bob Fleming, we flew to Tampa, rented a car and drove on to Fort Myers Beach. Catharine and Bob became increasingly concerned about my erratic driving - veering over the centre line into the path of eighteen-wheelers. Catharine concluded that the problem was exacerbated by Lithium, the medication I was on, and I have no doubt she was right.

I spent most of my time in Florida on a couch with the covers over my head. One night a fierce hurricane, an echo of the turmoil within me, struck the area and severely damaged nearby houses. Driving back to Tampa, I crashed the car into a tree, and at that point, despite my anger and resentment, Catharine took over the driving.

After we returned to Montreal, I immediately retreated to the safety of the couch. At my first appointment with Dr. Cervantes, Catharine, who always accompanied me, told the doctor about my erratic driving. He immediately changed the medication. The problem with most medication for clinical depression is that one must wait a month or more before the new drug kicks in and, of course, there is no guarantee it will work even then.

I continued to talk about suicide, spending a lot of time thinking about the procedure for obtaining a gun. On my couch, I also fantasized about arranging a suicide to appear as an accident. Obviously some remnant of the image of myself I had spent a lifetime so laboriously constructing was still important to me. My favourite scenario was to visit the Flemings at Madawaska in the Thousand Islands, go swimming in the St. Lawrence River and become caught in the swift current. According to Catharine, I became obsessed watching death scenes on television, although I don't remember that at all.

In fact, as I continued to plunge deeper into the black pit and the last glimmers of hope were snuffed out, there is more and more that I do not remember. Usually clinical depression lasts about eighteen months, so early in 1994, Dr. Cervantes, surprised and disappointed by my lack of response to a variety of medications including Prozac, consulted the director of in-patient psychiatric services at the Montreal General, Dr. Thomas Milroy. I then had an interview with Dr. Milroy in his office, an interview of which I remember nothing. Apparently at that time, Dr. Milroy was opposed to my being hospitalized. But in a subsequent visit with Dr. Cervantes, my gloom was so pervasive and my fears so palpable, I raised again the possibility of a course of treatment we had rejected before. I suggested we try electro-convulsive therapy.

On February 17, 1994, I exchanged my couch at home for a bed in the psychiatric ward on the fifth floor of the Montreal General. I remained there until March 10 although I was allowed to go home on weekends. I remember little of those three weeks. What I do remember most vividly was being wheeled to a large bright room early in the mornings where Dr. Milroy and his assistants would be ready and waiting. We would all politely say good morning and I would watch the bright sunlight dancing on the polished floor. Then cool hands would gently attach something to my temples and the next thing I would remember was being wheeled back to my room again.

There was no pain from the half dozen shock treatments I received. Also no benefit that I could discern. Apparently I resisted all other suggestions for help such as group therapy. I would only talk to one woman nurse, refused all visitors, and was extremely upset when a friend discovered I was there. So with nothing I could see to show for it, on March 10, I exchanged my bed in the psychiatric ward for my couch behind the drawn curtains at home.

From the onset of the depression in the early summer of 1992, Catharine was with me every step of the dreadful journey. She accompanied me to all the visits with Dr. Cervantes. She checked out treatment centres in the United States. She talked with friends such as

Marie and Andrew Foley in Boston who knew about depression. She consulted with anyone knowledgeable about the advisability of shock treatments. There was only so much she could do as my depression resisted treatment and deepened in the spring of 1994, but she kept trying. She would suggest I get up in the morning, but never badgered me about it. She would cook special savoury dishes, but never expressed disappointment when I refused to eat them. She would tell me about invitations from friends, but never complained when I refused to go. Outwardly through this whole ordeal, Catharine remained remarkably serene and it was only much later I realized how much it had drained her. During the months I have described, she felt we were both trying to withstand the powers of darkness, that our house was under siege and our home was filled with dark energy. She felt at times in the middle of a bombardment akin to *Star Wars*, with Luke Skywalker walking away down a long dark corridor to face the terrifying figure of Darth Vader. We were both involved in a cosmic struggle. It was clear to Catharine early on that the issue was life or death.

Catharine told me later that felt she was watching someone she loved walking along the edge of a cliff. But she was unable to call out a warning for fear I would fall off and plunge into the precipice. Often she would leave the house, sometimes at night, to escape the dark energy. Perhaps she would meet a neighbour walking her dogs. Just talking for a few minutes with the neighbour would give her a grasp on reality. She felt my depression was a kind of death experience for both of us, that no matter what happened in the end, our lives would never be the same again, that she had lost a home, a marriage and a husband.

Often I would say to Catharine that she would be better off without me. But if that happened, she told me, she would never hear my footsteps again, we would never sit down to supper together, we would never hold each other the way we once did. Catharine hung on to simple things for dear life, like the occasional flash of red in our back yard - two bright cardinals who had never been there before and who came almost every day. "Red messengers of God" Catharine called them. One day for an hour, she watched, transfixed, through the kitchen window, as they flitted in the snow. They gave her a sense of connection and reality in the midst of the storm.

Presently, though, Catharine realized she was powerless and couldn't save me, that ultimately I would have to do it myself. In the meantime, if she couldn't save me, she had to save herself. She left the house more, though she dreaded leaving. She spent more time with friends and joined a mutual-help group. Catharine knew that for me it could go either way, there was nothing more she could do. And she remembered the words of the General in the film, *Babette's Feast*: "Whatever choices we make, in the end there is only the infinite mercy of God."

By this time, March 1994, I had lost twenty pounds and aged as many years. Our dear friend, Clare Hallward, watching me shuffling down the steps, remarked to Catharine that I looked like an old man. In so many illnesses, even terminal ones, the patient retains hope for recovery. Not so with depression. At the core is the growing thought and finally the conviction that, one way or another, the only end is death. This does not mean that the desperation and the darkness are entirely unrelieved. Intermittently, a ray of relief would break through. But always the terror and the snarling dogs came back. I remember one morning not long before the end, terrified and paralyzed with fear, holding tightly onto Catharine in bed and saying in a strangled voice that I was scared and I didn't know what to do. I had never said words like that to anyone before. I didn't know it then but we were approaching the crisis.

Exactly a week before Good Friday in March 1994, a day soft and sunny, Catharine and I left Montreal and drove up the Laurentian Autoroute to the old monastery beside Rivière du Diable in Parc Mont Tremblant. We put on our cross-country skis in the parking lot and set off. I remember feeling almost exhilarated as we skied along through the pine trees, the wind in our face, the branches tracing tapestries on the snow which glittered in the sunshine.

Then Saturday morning I plunged again into a bottomless shaft of gloom and dread. I had never before felt so helpless and hopeless, so sunk in a curious state of perturbed paralysis. From my couch, I told Catharine I felt terrible, but she lived with her own dread and knew there was nothing she could do about mine. She had an appointment at Unitas, the meditation centre on Mount Royal above Pine Avenue, but was afraid to leave the house. However, in a way she could neither justify nor understand, she felt compelled to go. She locked the door behind her. I was alone.

I wanted to sink more deeply into the shaft of darkness and oblivion that would give me relief from this pain, this cancer of the soul. I wanted to sink into the soft nothingness of death. Suddenly, a flash like heat lightning lit up the oppressive gloom in my head. Momentarily I glimpsed the flames of hell and damnation flickering the way the Catholic Church had painted them to me as a little boy. I could feel the forbidden sex of my Jesuit years and taste the warming gurgle of alcohol melting the ice in my soul. Then the moment of clarity vanished. The clouds rolled in and the tapes in my head, the suicide tapes, began playing again.

I had long since given up the idea of a gun or death by drowning. The tape now playing was about a plunge onto the tracks of the Montreal métro. I knew this would be messy for me and for those who survived me, especially Catharine. But I was no longer thinking of others. My inner being was like an inkwell overflowing with black thoughts of nothing but myself.

I pushed off the blanket and got up from the couch, my body heavy and leaden. I watched my next movements as though I was a spectator in a dark cinema. Slowly and laboriously, I found a pencil and a piece of paper and wrote a one-sentence suicide note: "Dearest Catharine, I think you will be better off without me. Love, Neil." Then I folded the note, my own obituary notice, and placed it carefully on the floor just inside the front door.

It was a windy March day. I put on my parka, locked the front door and shuffled along to a bar on Sherbrooke Street. I thought it would be easier if I had a drink, although I had not had one in years. The world around me, the people, the cars, the stores with Easter decorations seemed unreal as if I was looking into a green-coloured fish tank. I sat at the bar for a few minutes but didn't order a drink. Then I trudged to the Vendôme métro station, just west of my home in Westmount. I walked down the steps into the métro, went out onto the apron and sat on a bench about twenty feet from the tracks. I stared glassily as about half a dozen trains roared by. Then I got up and went back home.

I think I was then, for just a moment, in a moment of calm - the eye of the storm. The physical activity of walking in the fresh cold air had briefly stilled the suicide tapes and given me just enough momentum to take a tiny positive step. Back home, I dialled the telephone number of my young friend, Chris, with whom I had breakfast occasionally. I don't know what the outcome would have been had he not answered. But he did and invited me to join him for supper at a neighbourhood restaurant. I agreed, went to the front door

143

and tore up the suicide note. The telephone rang. It was Catharine. I could hear the relief in her voice when I answered and when I told her I was having supper with Chris. Much later, she told me that about half an hour before, just when I was telephoning Chris, she somehow knew it was going to be all right. I asked her how she knew. She said she had been living such a stripped-down, fundamental existence that in a moment of unexpected clarity she felt in her innermost being that all would be well.

While picking at supper, I described for Chris as well as I could what a hell hole I had been in all day. Then with a kind of groan and in a strangled voice that came from deep inside me I said to him, "I just want to be real." Only six words, but they described and distilled a lifetime. I could no longer endure the split of feeling one way about myself but needing others to feel another way. I could no longer summon the energy to bear the mask to maintain that charade, no longer wanted to be a performer. I desperately wanted to be real and needed help to make the journey. Chris said he wanted me to go with him to meet a friend. Little did I realize this friend would guide me on a new journey and save my life.

15

SPIRITUAL AWAKENING

We drove several blocks, parked the car, walked up a flight of stairs to a mussy second-floor apartment swirling with cigarette smoke, where Chris introduced me to Jim. Jim was a man in his early sixties, medium height, with a moustache, a quizzical if not slightly sardonic expression on his face and the stub of a cigarette in his mouth. Jim lit another cigarette and invited me to come and sit at the kitchen table. I told him what I had told Chris at supper, "I just want to be real." Jim sensed immediately I was in a panic, perhaps needing professional help, and began to muse about a treatment centre, perhaps in the United States.

I pounded my fist on the kitchen table and said in desperation that I didn't have time to go looking for treatment places in the States - I needed help and I needed it right now! It was Jim's turn to pound the table. "All right," he said, "this is what we're going to do." Then, as though he was firing a machine gun, he laid out a program of activity that made my head swim - which is precisely what he intended. He wanted to change the tapes.

First, I was to come to his apartment, on foot, six nights a week at seven o'clock for a discussion; every evening before I came I was to sit down at my desk and write out a detailed agenda of my next day's activities; I was to fix a reasonable time for getting up in the morning and stick to it; I was to do at least an hour of physical exercise a day, preferably brisk walking; I was to watch for interesting films - to get me out of myself; I was to sign up for a weekend retreat with a group of Jim's friends - because their serenity and laughter might well be contagious; and I was to plant some kind of garden in my back yard so I could get real earth on my hands and stop and smell the roses (or, in the case of my garden, cherry tomatoes). And that wasn't all. Jim loaded me up with a stack of books to take home and read, most of them on some aspect of mental and emotional health, many of them based on the spirituality of twelve-step programs. I walked out the door that first night, with Jim's words ringing in my head: "You've been saying 'no' most of your life; try saying 'yes' more often."

As I walked home after that first meeting, I felt a twinge - almost imperceptible but still real - a twinge of hope. Jim had given me a down-to-earth program that I could begin immediately, and he also gave me the impression that if I didn't buckle down to it seriously, he would dump me. So I set my alarm clock for the morning, and to make doubly sure I would hit the deck running, I arranged to have breakfast as many mornings as possible with Chris in a nearby restaurant. I set aside time for the reading Jim gave me, checked the newspaper for entertaining films, went with Catharine to the Atwater Market to buy our tomato plants, and tried to say "yes" more often: for example, becoming involved with Benedict Labre House for Montreal's street people.

As the April weather became warmer I joined the Meadowbrook Golf Club in Montreal West. Frequently my good friend, Jean Prieur, would pick me up about 7:30 and we would play four hours of golf, no carts, walking briskly all the way. I arranged to take some lessons at Golf Gardens on Côte de Liesse and started to practise for the Madawaska Classic. This was the family golf tournament at Bob and Patsy Fleming's island summer home in the St. Lawrence near Gananoque, scheduled for the last weekend in August. Thanks to CJAD's news director, Gord Sinclair, I was still doing the afternoon radio program, only now I walked the dozen or so blocks to the station. Usually after I returned from CJAD, Catharine and I headed to the Westmount pool for a swim. At home again, I sat down at my desk and wrote out the next day's agenda, a simple enough task that steadied me and gave me reassurance like a security blanket.

And every evening after supper I set off for Jim's place on foot. Every time it was the same routine. First, we sat down in his den and watched videos, ranging from biblical archeology to the significance of myth, all raising questions about the meaning of life. As Jim told me much later, we were not seeking knowledge but wisdom; he wanted to find what made me tick; he wanted me to discover a new perception of reality. Then we moved to the living room where we listened to tapes, many of them relating to the spirituality of the twelve steps, most of them chock-a-block with humour. He wanted to see what made me laugh and what didn't. All I remember now is that for a long time, those tapes didn't.

And then we talked. Looking back now, it is difficult to remember all that we talked about - anger, resentment, arguments, anxiety, fear, shame. There was nothing theoretical about these discussions. Usually they were about my relationship with Catharine, with colleagues in the media, with the Jesuits and the Benedictines, with my father. If I didn't respond one night, Jim wouldn't push. Instead he would come at the same issue from another angle six nights later. Often we discussed incidents that had happened that very day, incidents that now seem inconsequential and picayune, but in fact revealed to Jim, and ultimately to me, patterns of behaviour and attitudes. How did I feel when Catharine asked me to get a loaf of bread? Did I usually open the car door for her? What triggered my last outburst of anger and did I see that it was a control issue?

Looking back on those many hours of discussion, I don't think what we talked about was nearly as important as my growing conviction that Jim understood me and what I had to do to change. He sensed what he called "the football of pain" in my stomach because he had dealt with it himself. He has a spacious and intellectually curious mind - he wants to do a study of the evolution of the Bible on his computer - but when it comes to everyday garden-variety spirituality, he is as down to earth and practical as a can opener. Time after time on those many evenings of two- or three-hour sessions, Jim astonished me at how accurately he could push the buttons that governed my emotional ups and downs. Sometimes he would use shock treatment: "You've spent a lot of your life being a pompous ass." Other times he would ask a simple question: "Do you think your attitude to Catharine is changing?" Presently I realized this was the key. Jim equated attitude change with personality change. My life had been soured by anxiety, fear, anger and resentment. There was little room for tranquillity, compassion, love, or real friendship.

So night after night we examined the inner dis-ease, trying to reduce the size of the football in my stomach. It was not easy going. Some days I would goof off, give up and head back to the security of the couch. On such an evening Jim would warn me, gently but firmly, that I was playing with fire, that we could lose all our hard-won gains in a moment of folly. Another time he was tougher. He asked me if I wanted to go back to the Vendôme métro station and, this time, jump.

When Dr. Cervantes heard about my suicide scenario he was extremely upset and rightly so. I had promised him I would contact him immediately about any suicide plans. He felt I had let him down, betrayed him, by keeping my plans to myself. Dr. Cervantes wanted me to go back into the hospital where I would be in a secure environment. I dreaded going back to the hospital and managed to convince the doctor to give me another chance. I think my fear of going back to the psychiatric ward provided a strong motive to keep me faithful to the program Jim had developed for me. And I added another element to the program. Despite my almost total lack of skill, and mindful of the dictum about starting to say yes instead of no, I joined a small group in an art class given by Jim's companion, Sharon, an effervescent woman whom I came to know and like. Little did I realize that for our final session I would be struggling to paint a live nude.

After a few weeks Jim had seized my attention ("pompous ass"), expanded my awareness (Catharine was astonished by my cooperation and thoughtfulness), and begun to shift my perception of reality to diminishing anger and resentment, growing serenity and compassion. In a way, Jim was helping me change the lenses through which I had viewed the world and this change was rooted in and related to a spiritual experience.

Because ultimately that is what the depression itself was, a fundamental spiritual experience. I had reached a spiritual and emotional crisis where, for a few critical and decisive hours, the emotions of despair and hope were balanced on a knife edge. There are, in my view, only two paths out of this existential crisis: giving up (some form of suicide) or giving in (some kind of surrender). The Chinese word for "crisis" has a double meaning, danger or opportunity, pointing the way to these two paths. Thanks to a strong instinct for survival which I have had all my life, with the help of divine providence and of many people, I chose to give in, to surrender.

What did I surrender and to whom? First and foremost, I surrendered control, a lifetime of trying to control the circumstances, the people, the success in my life. I even tried to control the most minute detail of daily living, such as boiling over with anger if Catharine was not at the door the minute we agreed to leave for an engagement. Further, I had to admit that I was powerless over my emotions of fear, anger and resentment, that in those areas my life had become unmanageable. I had to reach out beyond myself for help and had to surrender the front, the mask, the persona I had spent so many years laboriously constructing, the persona disguising how rotten I really felt about myself.

In biblical terms, I had to lose my life in order to find it. The depression had driven me to my knees. Jim told me to get on the floor each night before going to bed and each morning after rising and put the day in the hands of God - whether I believed in God or not. With a smile, Jim told me he knew people who were so shy about praying that even though they lived alone, they would go into the bathroom and lock the door before getting on their knees.

As a practical matter, I had no problem about getting on my knees or asking for help, even if I had to fake it until I made it. I knew full well I could not make myself well. So I had to reach out to a power greater than myself, and I had no trouble calling that power God. But I made a bargain with myself. Never again would I make a spiritual commitment that did not ring true, that was not real. I had been baptized and confirmed in the Roman Catholic Church, taken perpetual vows in the Jesuits, been ordained a priest. Never again would I take a step for which the map had been drawn by other people. So when the right time came, I knelt down with Jim in his smoke-filled living room, his Russian cat watching us, and made a decision to turn my will and my life over to the care of God as I understood God. I wasn't sure what the words meant or how the decision would turn out. But I had a good feeling about it.

As this program of activities, exercises and discussion continued through the spring and early summer of 1994, slowly, imperceptibly at first, my depression, like a fog on the landscape, began to lift. And I began to see and enjoy experiences - simple things I had not had for two years - a boat trip around the harbour, a sour-cream doughnut at Tim Horton's, a genuine spontaneous laugh from deep inside. This last was the best because I had not laughed for two years. One evening I went out into our back yard and excitedly picked my first cherry tomatoes, imagining how they would shine like red Christmas balls beside the poached salmon for dinner.

In July, Catharine and I drove to Prouts Neck on the coast of Maine where we spent ten days with Clare and John Hallward. In August we visited with Bob and Patsy Fleming at their hilltop summer house in the Thousand Islands. I was delighted to be named the most improved golfer in the "Madawaska Classic." I'm not sure what the accolade was based upon since I am one of those peculiar golfers who

149

never keeps score. I signed up to take and give a couple of courses at the McGill Institute for Learning in Retirement and at the Thomas More Institute. The fog was lifting, burned off by the warm sun of recovery.

People ask how I overcame my depression. There are, I think, three broad reasons for my recovery. The first is the treatment and support from the medical profession and other counsellors and therapists. This included psychotherapy, cognitive and group therapy, and counselling. I saw an insightful and understanding Jungian psychologist, Tom Kelly, for more than a year. I also had shock treatment and the very latest anti-depression medication.

I daresay I had access to the best treatment facility and medical personnel in North America at the Montreal General Hospital. The key person on the treatment team was the Director of the Mood Disorders Clinic, Dr. Pablo Cervantes. He is a remarkable, caring, intuitive, patient and skillful doctor. He never gave up when my depression, frustratingly and unpredictably, proved to be resistant to prolonged pharmacological treatment. In many ways Dr. Cervantes allowed me to manage my own treatment. He is a superb listener. He trusted me, and did not give up even after my suicide scenario. He paid attention to my wife and gave her support and hope. One day in his office, it was obvious to him the turnaround had begun, the snarling dogs were retreating and my depression was lifting. To my complete surprise, in a most uncharacteristic move, he jumped up in his chair and punched the air with a victory salute. I owe him a lot.

After the array of medical treatment, the second element in my recovery was daily physical exercise. I don't have any scientific way to explain how exercise affects our metabolism. But it seemed evident that striding around a golf course, the sun shining on the fairways and the birds chirping in the trees, beats lying in the dark on a couch, the blinds drawn and the covers pulled up over my head. And so it was with all the exercise during this recovery period - swimming, bicycling, golf, walking, gardening. Somehow all of it helped the body re-invigorate the psyche.

The third element in my recovery, by no means entirely dissociated from the medical and the physical, was the spiritual dimension. It was also, in my view, by far the most important and decisive. In his book *Simply Sane*, American psychiatrist Gerald May maintains that therapy alone will not save us or even change us. What did change some of his patients, Dr. May explains, was "some kind of deep spiritual existential experience." There is no doubt in my mind that for me this "deep spiritual existential experience" was triggered immediately by my depression, although three preceding events related in some way to the onset of the depression. These three events were my major chest surgery, regrets about my retirement from an exciting career in the media, and profound sadness about the distressing breakup of the meditation community at the Benedictine Priory.

It is immediately evident that all these experiences share a common element - a sense of something being lost, with its concomitant feeling of grief. This sense of loss is also emphasized in William Styron's memoir on depression. Still, these events were only the occasion of my depression, not its cause. I believe that the cause was a lifetime of chronic anxiety, fear, resentment, anger, alienation, shame, loneliness, success, religious strictures, public acclaim, sex and alcohol - which almost destroyed me.

These are the main elements of my depression, but they are not its positive dynamics. How can the elements of a life-threatening disease be transformed into steps of recovery? How can the change from depression to recovery be effected? What is the nature of the "deep spiritual existential experiences" that Dr. Gerald May posits as essential to getting well?

Obviously this existential experience involves at its base a fundamental change. But what kind of change? It is easier to describe what the change is not than what it is. It is not only an external change. It will not be enough to win the lottery or take a holiday at Banff or move to Florida or California. It will not be enough to make new friends or even form a serious relationship with another person and count on him or her to make you feel better. The kind of change I am talking about will not come through a promotion at work or being awarded the Order of Canada.

All these are external changes. They change our circumstances. They do not change the core of our being - where we live, where the discomfort and the dis-ease are located. These changes are only cosmetic. They do not reach the inner person. The image I present to the world may be as smooth and shining as a rosy apple. The trouble is that when the apple is cut, part of the core is wormy and rotten. So underneath our gleaming exterior, our core and centre may be diseased and unhealthy and no external change will cure it, because our inner disease is part and parcel of us, of who we really are.

151

What is this inner disease? What are its major elements? Basically, the disease is characterized by fear - fear that, no matter how successful we are, we have never measured up, that we are not good enough, that, in fact, we are failures. We have never measured up to our parents, our teachers, our priest, minister, rabbi, our church. And we never measured up to what God expects of us or what we were told God expects of us. We have failed them all and the result is we don`t much like ourselves. At the core of our being, no matter how polished and successful our exterior, is the worm of self-hatred, self-loathing.

And this points the way to the nature of the change and why a change that is merely external will never suffice for any length of time. Very simply we must change from disliking ourselves to liking ourselves. In my view this is the most basic change there is at the emotional, psychological and spiritual level. The next question is key: how can this existential spiritual change be brought about? Not easily. Not by reading a book or taking a course. Not by a relationship, no matter how intense.

I believe the only phenomenon that can bring about this existential spiritual change is a crisis of some sort or other. In my case the crisis took the form of a severe and prolonged clinical depression. The depression could have driven me to give up or give in. Giving up would likely have meant suicide which I seriously considered. Giving in meant some kind of surrender to something or somebody greater than myself. In my case, it meant getting on my knees, admitting honestly there were aspects of my life I could not control and, again honestly, reaching out and asking for help.

In some mysterious paradoxical way, admitting that I had lost control and could not manage myself without help, enabled healing to begin. I think the key here is the willingness to give in and surrender. Because that act of humility - or down-to-earth reality which is what humility means - cuts through the control issue the way a hot knife cuts through butter. And once we have shaken off our back the "control monkey," which we have carried for years, the process of healing can really begin.

At the heart of this process of healing, of moving from loathing ourselves to liking ourselves, is a paradox. When we do give up control, when we admit that we cannot handle the situation and reach out for help, when we make ourselves vulnerable and open to being wounded, then and only then can we be healed. When we are most vulnerable to external threats which we have feared all our lives, then, in a paradoxical way, we have made ourselves most available for healing. As the Jungian analyst Marian Woodman writes, "God comes through the wound."

So the existential spiritual journey from disliking ourselves to liking ourselves can be a short journey, but it is a difficult one because it is weighed down by the garbage of a lifetime. The admission of helplessness, the giving up of control, the plea for help, the risk of vulnerability, the healing, are all parts of the journey. And in my case, it involved finding a guide who could help me find my way. Much of Jim's guidance came from his own deep familiarity with the spirituality of Alcoholics Anonymous as articulated in the twelve steps. I had read somewhere that Scott Peck, author of *The Road Less Traveled*, considered AA the most significant spiritual development of this century. I began to understand why this was so as Jim and I talked about elements in the twelve steps and how they related to the process of recovery. These steps are a program for living that would enrich the life of anyone, addict or not, and I believe that in one way or another we are all addicts. We are all trying to fill a spiritual vacuum with success, money, relationships, fame, alcohol or drugs.

Or as Scott Peck puts it: "We are all wounded. None of us really has it all together. None of us can really go it alone. We are all in need, in crisis, although most of us still seek to hide the reality of our brokenness from ourselves and from one another. The men and women of AA ... must confess their brokenness ... and in that sense alcoholism may be a blessing." Or to put it another way, the spirituality of the twelve steps is relevant as a program of living for anyone on the journey. The three basic elements in twelve-step spirituality that worked for me and might be universally helpful are: an admission of being powerless, a willingness to give up control, and a reaching out for help to a power greater than oneself. I think this is a formula for healing and becoming whole. At any rate, it was for me.

All that I have been describing as a transformation from interior discomfort and dis-ease to a degree of comfort and wholeness, from loathing ourselves to liking ourselves, even in a mild way, is not a proposition but a process. It takes time. It involves not only a goal but a journey. Or as Henry Miller put it: "Our destination is never a place but a new way of looking at things." All the time I was working with Jim, he was interested in whether my attitude was changing, if I was seeing

Catharine and my work and even my resentments in a new way. One beautiful morning on the golf course - the sun was out, the birds were singing - I said to one of my fellow-golfers that it was a lovely morning. "Indeed it is," he replied, "but we'll pay for it." A simple remark, but we were seeing the world through different lenses.

No one, I think, has put this more strikingly than T.S. Eliot in *Little Gidding*:

> We shall not cease from exploration
> And the end of all our exploring
> Will be to arrive where we started
> And know the place for the first time.

In the process that Jim took me through, I began to see my world and feel about it in a different way. The lonely, anxious little boy sitting on the steps of my father's hardware store in Hastings had changed. In a moment of profound crisis when I had admitted to myself I was helpless, I reached out and there was someone there. In that very act, totally honest and real, healing began. The interior split between the way I felt about myself and the way I wanted others to feel about me, began to diminish. I gave up the obsessive drive to control. From being fragmented and torn apart inside, I started to feel more whole - a theme that is elaborated in one of my favourite books, *The Spirituality of Imperfection*, by Ernest Kurtz and Catherine Ketcham. For the first time in my life the ball was hitting the glove, the arrow the target. I felt I was fitting, connecting in a way I never had before with myself, with other people, and with my understanding of God.

Perhaps I should say a word here about God as I understand God. I have always believed and still believe that there is something bigger than me in the universe or as someone said, "There is a God and you're not it." Of course I can't prove there is a God. But even at the rational level I think the existence of this world makes more sense with a God than without one. I believe there is an after-life and the way we live here will affect the way we will live there. I do not censure one iota those who do not or cannot believe in God. I say only, realizing all the while that faith is a gift, that I am a believer and pray I remain so till my earthly end. I cannot put this better than the writer Morris West: "I have learned to be grateful for the small candle that lights my own faltering steps and to hope that when it gutters out, I may wake to a final illumination."

Of course, no one else will relate to God just as I do (I still consider myself a practising Roman Catholic) and some will not relate to God at all. Nor do I think everyone must go through an experience of depression such as mine to become more whole. What I do think is that many people are not comfortable in their skin and are seeking ways to relieve their discomfort, often trying to fill a spiritual vacuum with material reality. And I think we must lose our life in order to find it. What I had to lose was my obsessive need to control. This need was so pervasive, so imbedded in my bones, that a spiritual crisis had to occur in order for me to fall on my knees and ask for help. Such a crisis need not be clinical depression. But whatever it is, it must be an experience that transforms the way we feel about ourselves and the way we perceive the world. It will involve relying on a power greater than ourselves whom some people call God. It will almost certainly involve some practice of habitual prayer. And by prayer I mean only a simple and honest reaching out of the human heart toward whatever power there may be at the foundation of life.

It was my birthday, New Year's Eve 1994, about six months after my depression had lifted for good and after the happiest summer of my life. Catharine and I had spent the afternoon cross-country skiing and were relaxing before supper in the lounge of the Laurentian Lodge Club at Prévost, amid the soft rolling foothills of the Laurentians. Outside the frosted windows, the moonlight was glittering on a fresh snowfall; inside, a roaring fire flamed up the chimney of the large stone fireplace. At a splendid dinner prepared by our talented chef, André, I was presented with a birthday cake and a rousing chorus of "Happy Birthday" to mark my threescore years and ten.

Naturally I thought that was the end of it. Imagine my surprise when a group of club members went to the front of the room and put on a mélange of songs, skits and humorous sketches in my honour. They had been working on the show all day. One skit especially brought the house down. I (that is, my impersonator) was about to hit a golf ball. Another golfer rushed up to warn me: "Stop! You're hitting from the ladies' tee!" I waved the other golfer away with exasperation. "This," I replied, "is my second shot!"

I don't ever remember feeling happier. I felt connected in a way I had never felt connected before to these people who were my friends. I laughed, and it was a genuine laugh. In some measure, I had become real. I was comfortable in my skin. And as I sat there in the dancing light of the fireplace and the happy sounds of singing, I thought of all the people including my family and the Jesuits and my friends who had helped me on my journey. I thought of how God does indeed write straight with crooked lines. And then I thought, with Catharine smiling beside me, the best is yet to be.

SHORELINE

Vi Bercovitch • Mirror, Mirror, *Terse Verse for Seasoned Citizens*

M. Laurel Buck • Stream of Memory, *Reflections of Megantic County*

A. Margaret Caza • Walk Alone Together, *Portrait of a French-English Marriage*
• The Lights of Lancaster, *Letters to Rome*

Eugenie Doucet • Tapas, *A Spanish Interlude*

Dennis Dwyer • Beyond Jargon, *What you need to know about Mediation - A Canadian Perspective*

Dwyer, Cadham & Letourneau • Bent but not Broken, *Today's Canadian Church*

Judith Isherwood • Down to Earth
• A Historical Walking Tour of Ste-Anne-de-Bellevue
• Tickets, *A Play in One Act*

Eve McBride • Dandelions Help

Sharen McDonald • A Gentleman and a Scholar

Neil McKenty • The Inside Story, *Journey of a former Jesuit priest and talk show host towards self-discovery*

Leslie Allison Minturn • Mildred Minturn, *A Biography*

Vera Gauley Munro • The September Years

Bess Burrows Rivett • Looking Back

Susan Romvary • Zsuzsa not Zsazsa, *Balance with a Smile*

Anna Woods • Healing Waters, *The Mayan Series*

Shulamis Yelin • Shulamis, *Scenes from a Montreal Childhood*

160